PITMAN'S
SHORTHAND MANUAL

NEW ERA EDITION

19

PITMAN'S
SHORTHAND
MANUAL

(BEING PART 1 OF PITMAN'S SHORTHAND INSTRUCTOR)

AN EXPOSITION OF
SIR ISAAC PITMAN'S
SYSTEM OF SHORTHAND

NEW ERA EDITION

Isaac Pitman

LONDON
SIR ISAAC PITMAN & SONS, LTD., PARKER STREET, W.C.2
BATH: PHONETIC INSTITUTE
MELBOURNE: THE RIALTO, COLLINS STREET
TORONTO: 70 BOND STREET
NEW YORK: 2 WEST 45TH STREET

PRINTED IN GREAT BRITAIN
AT THE PITMAN PRESS, BATH

PREFACE

THE system of shorthand writing presented in the following pages was invented by Sir Isaac Pitman, who in 1837 published his first treatise on the art. In 1840 the second edition of his work appeared, under the title " Phonography, or Writing by Sound, being also a New and Natural System of Shorthand." In the numerous editions of Phonography published in succeeding years, many improvements were introduced. These were the fruit of long and varied stenographic experiments, and of the valuable criticism and experience of large numbers of expert writers of the system who had applied it to work of every description. No other system of shorthand designed for the English language has been subjected to tests so prolonged, so diverse, and so severe as those which Pitman's Shorthand—as the system is now generally styled —has undergone during the last eighty-six years, with the result that it has been most successfully adapted to the practical requirements of all classes of shorthand writers.

The present edition includes a few alterations that have been made in certain rules of the system. The effect of these alterations is to simplify the work of the student without in any way interfering with the wonderful power of the system in the hands of the expert writer. The object specially borne in mind in preparing the work has been to render it equally suitable for self-tuition and for individual or class instruction under a teacher. No effort has been spared to explain and illustrate the rules in the clearest and simplest manner possible.

Although students, as a rule, experience no difficulty in understanding the method here set forth of "writing by sound," it is desirable that they should have, at the beginning of their study, an intelligent grasp of all that is conveyed by that term. Therefore, before the mastery of the first chapter is attempted, the Introduction which follows this Preface should be read with care.

The advantage of practical ability in the art of shorthand writing is so universally acknowledged in the present day that it is unnecessary to emphasize it. It is obvious, however, that the value of shorthand, whether as a vehicle for private communication or for use in various ways in business or professional life, would be largely diminished if the same system—and that the best—were not employed. This important fact is now generally recognized ; and statistics, the testimony of public men, and general observation, concur in demonstrating that the system which Sir Isaac Pitman invented is taught and used as the shorthand *par excellence* for all who speak the English language. Further and very significant evidence to the merits of his system is the fact that it has been adapted to no fewer than twenty foreign languages.

The Publishers take this opportunity of tendering their sincere thanks to the large number of expert writers and teachers of Phonography who have offered valuable suggestions for the improvement of the present edition.

INTRODUCTION

PHONOGRAPHY, the name originally given to Pitman's Shorthand, has been briefly but accurately defined as " the art of representing spoken sounds by character ; a system of shorthand." The first question that will occur to the student will be, what is the fundamental difference between the shorthand characters and the letters in ordinary writing and printing ? To answer this question it is necessary to consider the alphabet of the language. It is obvious that the usual or Romanic alphabet of twenty-six letters cannot represent by distinct characters the thirty-six typical sounds of the English language. As a consequence, many of the letters of that alphabet are of necessity used to represent different sounds. It is manifest, therefore, that any system of shorthand founded on the common alphabet would prove a very imperfect and cumbrous instrument for recording spoken utterances with certainty and speed—the chief object of shorthand. With such an alphabet either a single sign standing for one of the letters would be required to do duty for several sounds, or more than one character would have to be used to represent a single sound, as is done in ordinary spelling. On the other hand, the three consonants C, Q and X are unnecessary, inasmuch as they represent sounds provided for by other consonants. Two simple illustrations will demonstrate the difference between the ordinary spelling and the phonetic method, which is the distinctive feature of Pitman's Shorthand.

The first illustration deals with consonants, and is concerned with the ordinary spelling of the words *gaol* and *gale*, in which the *sounds* of the first consonant are different, although represented in longhand by the same letter. If the common spelling were followed in shorthand, we should have the same shorthand symbols for both words. But the initial sounds in these words are different; in the first the sound is *jay*, in the second *gay*. For these dissimilar sounds the Pitman system provides dissimilar shorthand signs. The second illustration deals with vowels, as, for example, in the words *tub* and *tube*. If the shorthand symbols were the equivalents of the letters of the common alphabet (the final *e* of *tube* being omitted because it is not sounded), the stenographer would be obliged to write both words by precisely the same characters, namely, *t-u-b*. Pitman's Shorthand, however, provides for the representation of the different sounds *ŭ* and *ū* heard in the respective words, and these are indicated by different symbols.

The phonetic notation of the system of shorthand developed in the present work has been found, after widely extended use, to possess important practical advantages. By the employment of the phonetic alphabet, which has been termed the " alphabet of nature," spoken language can be recorded with one-sixth of the trouble and time that longhand requires, by those who use Pitman's Shorthand simply as a substitute for the ordinary longhand writing. With the adoption of the systematized methods of abbreviation developed in the more advanced stages, this method of shorthand can be written legibly with the speed of the most rapid distinct articulation, and it may be read with the certainty and ease of ordinary longhand writing.

An explanation on one point, however, is desirable. In the study and use of Pitman's Shorthand it should be borne in mind that although the system is phonetic it is not designed to represent or record minute shades of pronunciation. The Pitmanic alphabet, in the words of Max-Müller, " comprehends the thirty-six broad typical sounds of the English language and assigns to each a definite sign." It does not seek to mark, for example, the thirty or more variations of sound which have been found to exist in the utterance of the twelve simple vowels. The pronunciation of the vowels, as Max-Müller has shown, varies greatly in different localities and in the various countries of the world in which the English language is spoken, and in which Pitman's Shorthand is practised. The standard of pronunciation, as exhibited in printed shorthand, cannot, therefore, be expected to coincide minutely with the pronunciation of English in all parts. Experience has abundantly proved that the representation of the broad typical sounds of English as provided for in Pitman's Shorthand is ample for all stenographic purposes.

The pronunciation adopted in Pitman's Shorthand Textbooks is based on that given in *The Oxford English Dictionary*, edited by Sir James A. H. Murray, LL.D.

The presence of *r* has a modifying effect upon a preceding vowel. The student's attention is, therefore, directed to the following observations with regard to the consonant *r*, to certain vowels when preceding *r* and to a class of vowels which may be described as more or less obscure.

(*a*) With the exception of *worsted* (the woollen material) and a few proper names, as *Worcester*, wherever the consonant *r* occurs in a word, in Pitman's Shorthand it must be *represented as a consonant*.

(*b*) In such words as *bar*, *far*, *mar*, *tar*, *jar*, the vowel-sign for *ah* is to be used ; but in such words as *barrow*, *Farrow*, *marry*, *carry*, and *Jarrow*, the first vowel-sound is to be represented by the vowel-sign for *ă*.

(c) In such words as *four, fore, roar, lore, wore, shore, door, pour, core, gore, tore, sore,* the vowel-sign for ō is to be used.

(d) In such words as *torch, morn, fork,* the vowel-sign for ŏ is to be used.

(e) In such words as *air, fair, lair, bare,* the vowel-sign for ā is to be used.

(f) In such pairs of words as *fir, fur ; earth, worth ; per, purr ; Percy, pursy ;* the vowel-sound in the first word of the pairs is to be represented by the vowel-sign for ĕ ; the vowel-sound in the second word of the pairs is to be represented by the vowel-sign for ŭ.

(g) In words like *custody, custom, baron, felony, colour, factory,* the second vowel-sound is represented by the vowel-sign for ŭ.

(h) In words like *village, cottage, breakage,* the second vowel-sound is represented by the vowel-sign for ĕ.

(i) In words like *suppose,* the second vowel-sound is represented by the vowel-sign for ō ; but in words like *supposition, disposition,* the second vowel-sound is represented by the vowel-sign for ŭ.

With the accurate employment of the phonographic signs, there need be no uncertainty as to what those employed for a particular word are intended to represent, and, as Max-Müller has testified, "English can be written rationally and read easily" with the Pitmanic alphabet. To use Pitman's Shorthand successfully, the rules of the system must be thoroughly mastered. By the employment of the various abbreviating devices, the most important benefit to be derived from shorthand will be attained, namely, the maximum of speed combined with legibility.

DIRECTIONS TO THE STUDENT

The system of shorthand set forth in the following pages received the name of Phonography (a term derived from two Greek words meaning " sound writing ") because it affords the means of recording the sounds of spoken language. From the outset, therefore, the student should remember that he is learning to write by SOUND, *i.e.*, to write words as they are pronounced ; that each simple character represents one definite sound and no other ; and that the ordinary spelling—with its many irregularities and inconsistencies—as exhibited in printing and in longhand writing, is not to be followed or imitated.

When the student has mastered the value of the phonographic signs, he should use those which represent the equivalent sounds in forming the characters for the words he desires to write. For example, if he wishes to write in Phonography the word *knee* (spelt with four letters, though made up of only two sounds), he uses but two phonographic signs, namely, that for the consonant *n* and that for the vowel *ē*. To spell in this fashion, a mental analysis of the sounds of words must be made, but the ability to do this is very easily acquired, and is soon exercised without conscious effort.

For working the exercises and for ordinary phonographic writing, a pen and ruled paper should be used. Speaking generally, it is not so easy to acquire a neat style of writing by the use of a pencil as it is by the use of a pen. No doubt, the pencil is frequently employed ; in some cases, indeed, it may be found impossible to use a pen for note-taking. The student would do well, therefore, to accustom himself to write either with a pen or a pencil in the more advanced stages of his progress, though for writing the exercises given in this book the pen only should be used.

The pen should be held lightly, and in such a manner as to permit of the shorthand characters being easily written. The wrist must not be allowed to rest upon the note-book or desk. In order to secure the greatest freedom of movement, the middle of the fore-arm should rest on the edge of the desk. The writer should sit in front of his work, and should have the paper or note-book parallel with the edge of the desk or table. For shorthand writing, the nib employed should not be too stiff, but should have a sufficiently fine and flexible point to enable the thick and thin characters of the system to be written so as clearly to distinguish the one from the other. Paper with a fairly smooth surface is absolutely essential.

The student should thoroughly master the explanations and rules which precede the respective exercises, and write out several times the illustrative words appearing in the text, afterwards working the exercises. As the secret of success in shorthand is PRACTICE, it is advisable that the various exercises should be written and re-written until they can be done with perfect freedom and accuracy. The perusal of progressive reading lessons in printed shorthand will also be found helpful to the student in forming a correct style of writing; and the practice of writing the characters, at first with careful accuracy, afterwards with gradually accelerated speed, will materially assist him in forming a neat style of shorthand writing.

The system is fully explained in the following pages, and can be acquired from the instruction books alone by anyone who is prepared to devote ordinary perseverance and application to the study. With the assistance of a teacher, however, more rapid and satisfactory advance will be made in the mastery of the art. Should any difficulty be experienced in finding a teacher, the publishers will be pleased to furnish any student with the names and addresses of the nearest teachers of Pitman's Shorthand. It should be pointed out that satisfactory progress in acquiring the art of shorthand will only be made if a certain portion of time is regularly devoted to the study EVERY DAY ; or, in the case of school or class instruction, by a thorough and punctual performance of the allotted portions of work forming the course. Study at irregular intervals of time is of little value; but an hour, or a longer period, devoted daily to the task will give the student a knowledge of the system in a comparatively short time, and constant and careful practice will bring speed and dexterity.

CONTENTS

KEY TO PITMAN'S
SHORTHAND MANUAL
New Era Edition

Containing a Key to the Exercises
Price 9d.

PITMAN'S SHORTHAND
(PHONOGRAPHY)

CHAPTER I
THE CONSONANTS

" Consonants are the result of audible friction or stopping of the breath in some part of the mouth or throat." (*Prof. Sweet.*)

Forms of Consonants. 1. For the representation of all the consonant sounds, (except *w*, *y*, and the aspirate *h*), the simplest geometrical forms are used, namely, the straight line and the shallow curve, as shown in the following diagrams—

Arrangement of Groups. 2. The order of the arrangement of each group of consonants, as exhibited in the Table on a following page, follows the order of the oral movements from the lips inwards in the utterance of their respective sounds. The first pair of consonants, *p*, *b*, are pronounced between the lips, and the next seven pairs at the several barriers further back in the mouth, in the succession indicated in the phonographic alphabet.

Classes of Consonants. 3. The first eight consonants, represented by straight strokes, are called " explodents," because, in pronouncing them, the outgoing breath is forced in a sudden gust through barriers previously closed.

4. The next eight, represented by upright or sloping curves, are called " continuants," because in uttering these the outgoing breath, instead of being

expelled suddenly, is allowed to escape in a continuous stream through similar barriers partially open.

5. The "nasals," represented by a horizontal curve, are produced by closing the successive barriers in the mouth against the outgoing air-stream, so that it has to escape through the nose.

6. The "liquids" flow into union with other consonants, and thus make double consonants, as in the words *cliff*, *dry*, where the *l* or *r* blends with the preceding consonant.

7. The "coalescents" precede vowels and coalesce or unite with them.

8. The "aspirate" is a breathing upon a following vowel. Thus by a breathing upon the vowel *ă* in the word *at*, the word is changed into *hat*.

Pairs of Consonants. 9. The first sixteen consonants form pairs; thus, *p* and *b*; *t* and *d*; *ch* and *j*; *k* and *g*; *f* and *v*; *th* and *th*; *s* and *z*; *sh* and *zh*. The articulations in these pairs are the same, but the sound is light in the first consonant of each pair and heavy in the second. The consonants of each pair are represented by the same stroke, but for the second consonant this is written *thick* instead of *thin*; as ╲ *p*, ╲ *b*, │ *t*, │ *d*, ╰ *f*, ╰ *v*, etc. We have, therefore, a *light sign* for the *light sound*, and a *heavy sign* for the *heavy sound*. In this, as in the fact that each pair of consonants is represented by kindred signs, a natural relation is preserved between the *spoken* sound and the *written* sign. Throughout this book whatever relates to the light strokes applies also to the corresponding heavy strokes unless the contrary is stated.

Size of Strokes. 10. The consonants should be written about one-sixth of an inch long, as in these pages. It is of the utmost importance that from the

outset the student should learn to form the whole of
the strokes uniformly as to length. Whatever size be
adopted, all the strokes should be made equal in length.
Later there will be introduced a principle for writing
strokes half the normal length, and later still another
for the making of strokes double the normal length.
It is thus imperative that the student should obtain
a fixed and strictly uniform length from the start.
Care should be taken to form the curved thick letters,
when standing alone, thus ⌣ v,) z. If made
heavy throughout they look clumsy : they should
be thick in the middle only, and should taper off at
each end, except when a joining such as ⌣ v g
or ⌣ b ng is made. Thick strokes are never
written upward. As an aid to remembering the
strokes for *th* and *s*, the student should note that
) s is the curve on the right side of ⌣ The
consonants *l* and *r* form the *l*eft and *r*ight sides of
an arch ⌢ The consonant *l* is most commonly
written upwards ; but it may be written downward
in certain cases in accordance with rules which will
be explained later.

Names of Consonants. 11. Until the student is
perfectly familiar with the names of the consonants
and the characters representing them, he should,
in writing out the exercises, name aloud each
shorthand stroke as he writes it. The strokes must
always be called by their phonetic names : thus,
" ch " is to be named *chay ;* " g " *gay ;* " ng " *ing.*
The reason for this is that each phonetic character
has a fixed value, and, therefore, requires to be called
by a name which indicates the sound that it invariably
represents.

Divisions	Character	Name	Letter	As sounded in
Explodents	╲	pee	P	**p**ost ro**p**e
	╲	bee	B	**b**oast ro**b**e
	│	tee	T	**t**ip fa**t**e
	│	dee	D	**d**ip fa**d**e
	╱	chay	CH	**ch**est e**tch**
	╱	jay	J	**j**est e**dg**e
	—	kay	K	**c**ane lee**k**
	—	gay	G	**g**ain lea**g**ue
Continuants	⌣	ef	F	**f**at sa**f**e
	⌣	vee	V	**v**at sa**v**e
	(	ith	TH	**th**igh wrea**th**
	(	thee	*TH*	**th**y wrea**th**e
	)	ess	S	**s**eal ba**s**e
	)	zee	Z	**z**eal bai**z**e
	⌣	ish	SH	**sh**e da**sh**
	⌣	zhee	ZH	trea**s**ure vi**si**on
Nasals	⌢	em	M	**m**et see**m**
	⌣	en	N	**n**et see**n**
	⌣	ing	NG	ki**ng**ly lo**ng**
Liqüids	⌣ up	el	L	**l**ight ti**l**e
	⌣ up down	ar, ray	R	**r**ight ti**r**e
Coalescents	╱ up	way	W	**w**et a**w**ay
	╱ up	yay	Y	**y**et a**y**ah
Aspirate	◦ up down	hay	H	**h**igh ad**h**ere

Exercise 1

(To be written by the student. The arrow »—→ shows the direction in which the stroke is to be written. The curves m, n and ng and the straight strokes k and g are written on the line.)

P, B

T, D

CH, J
(chay)

K, G
(gay)

F, V

TH, *TH*
(ith) (thee)

S, Z
(zee)

SH, ZH
(ish) (zhee)

M

N

NG
(ing)

L

R

R
(ray)

W
(way)

Y
(yay)

H
(hay)

Chay and Ray. 12. These strokes are somewhat similar. They differ, however, in slope and in the direction in which they are written. It is scarcely possible, moreover, to mistake one for the other, inasmuch as *chay* is always written DOWN at an angle of 30° from the perpendicular, and *ray* is always written UP at an angle of 30° from the horizontal; thus ⟋ *chay*, ⟋ *ray*. If the pupil cannot, at the first trial, produce a fair copy of the signs in Exercise 1, he should write them several times, and vary the practice by writing the strokes in irregular order; thus,

Exercise 2

Read, copy and transcribe as shown in line 1

1. ＼ ＼ | | / ／ ＿ ＿ ⟍ ⟋ ? ⟋ ⟋
    p b t d ch j k g w y h h r

2. ⟋ ＼ ⟋ | ? ＼ ⟋ | / ⟋ ＿ / ＿

3. ⟍ ⟍ ⟍ (( )) ⟍ ⟍ ⌒ ⌒ ⌣ ⌒

4. ⟋ ⌒ ⟍ ⟍ ⟍ (⌣) ⌒ (⟍ ⟍ ⌣)

5. ＼ (⟋ ⌒ | / ⟋) ⌣ ⟍) | |

6. ＼ ＿ ? ⟍ ⟋ / ⟋ ＿ ⟋ ⟍ ⟋ ＿ |

7. ⟍ ⟍) (⌒ ⌣ ⟍ ⟍ ( ) ⟍ ⌒

8. | ＿ ＿ | ＿ ＼ / ＼ / / ? ⟋ ⟋ ⟋ /

Joined Strokes. 13. Strokes when joined must be written without lifting the pen, the beginning of a following stroke joining the end of a preceding stroke, as in the following exercise.

Exercise 3

Read and copy

1.

p,　pt,　pd,　p ch,　pj,　pk.

2.

bf,　d th,　ds,　ch s,　jm,　jl,　lm.

3.

kl,　km,　kn,　kk,　kd.

4.

fr,　frl,　frld,　fl,　f ch,　fj.

5.

th m,　th l,　th r,　th rfr,　sk,　lk.

6.

sh p,　sh bl,　sh k,　sh r,　sh rl,　sh m.

7.

hd,　hv,　h th,　hn,　hb,　h ch.

Exercise 4

Read, copy, and transcribe

1.

2.

3.

4.

5.

6.

The student will see the correct angles for the upright and sloping characters if he will copy and practise the following forms in combination—

Summary

1. Pitman's Shorthand is phonetic, words being written according to their sound.
2. The strokes are twenty-six in number, and each stroke has a distinct name and value.
3. To represent the consonants there are mainly two elements, a straight stroke and a shallow curve.
4. The strokes (straight and curved) are thin and thick for the representation of pairs of similar sounds.
5. Thin strokes are written sometimes upward, sometimes downward ; thick strokes are never written upward.
6. Strokes must be of a uniform length, about one-sixth of an inch.
7. Strokes are written by one impression, and the thick curves taper at each end.
8. The stroke representing *chay* is written downward ; the stroke representing *ray* is written upward.
9. Strokes when joined must be written without lifting the pen.

CHAPTER II

THE VOWELS

" If the mouth-passage is left so open as not to cause audible friction, and voiced breath is sent through it, we have a vowel." (*Prof. Sweet.*)

Vowel Sounds. 14. There are six simple long vowel-sounds in the English language, namely—

$$ah, \quad \bar{a}, \quad \bar{e}\,; \quad aw, \quad \bar{o}, \quad \bar{oo}\,;$$
as heard in the words
bah! āle, ēach; āll, ōāk, ōōze.

15. There are six corresponding short vowel-sounds in the language, namely—

$$\breve{a}, \quad \breve{e}, \quad \breve{i}, \quad \breve{o}, \quad \breve{u}, \quad \breve{oo}$$
as heard in the words
ăt, ĕtch, ĭt, ŏdd, tŭb, bŏŏk.

The long vowels may be remembered by repeating the sentence " *Pa may we all go too ?* " The short vowels may be remembered by repeating the sentence " *That pen is not much good.*"

Vowel Signs. 16. The long vowels are represented by a heavy dot and a heavy dash. The short vowels are represented by a light dot and a light dash.

Vowel Places. 17. There are three places close to each stroke where a vowel sign may be placed, namely, at the beginning, the middle, and the end. The vowels are accordingly called first-place, second-place, and third-place vowels respectively.

The places of the vowels are counted from the point where the stroke begins. In the case of down-strokes, therefore, the vowel places are counted from the top downward. In the case of upstrokes, the

9

vowel places are counted from the bottom upward.
In the case of horizontals, the vowel places are
counted from left to right ; thus,

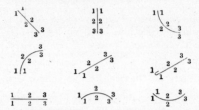

Value of Vowel-Signs. 18. The vowel-signs are
put in the places which correspond with their numbers.
A heavy dot in the first-place represents the long
vowel *ah* ; in the second-place it represents the long
vowel *ā* ; in the third-place it represents the long
vowel *ē*. A heavy dash in the first place represents
the long vowel *aw* ; in the second place it represents the
long vowel *ō* ; in the third place it represents the
long vowel *ōō*.

19. The light vowel-signs for the short vowels
are put in the same places as the heavy vowel-signs
for the long vowels ; thus,

calm.	*Cam,*	*bait,*	*bet,*	*eel,*	*ill.*
pawed.	*pod,*	*rote,*	*rut,*	*pool,*	*pull.*
Paul,	*Polly.*	*coal.*	*cull,*	*peel,*	*pill.*
fade.	*fed,*	*raid,*	*red,*	*dome,*	*dumb.*

Vowels preceding and following Strokes. 20. When a vowel-sign is placed on the left-hand side of an upstroke or downstroke, it is read *before* the stroke, as ⟋ *ale,* ⟋ *earth,* ⟍ *ape,* ⟋ *age,* � *eat.*

When a vowel-sign is placed on the right-hand side of an upstroke or downstroke, it is read *after* the stroke, as ⟋ *lay,* ⟋ *ray,* ⟍ *pay,* ⟋ *jay,* ⟋ *shoe.*

When a vowel-sign is placed above a horizontal stroke it is read *before* the stroke, as ‒‧ *ache,* ‒‧ *eke,* ⌣ *own.*

When a vowel-sign is placed below a horizontal stroke it is read *after* the stroke, as ‒‧ *Kay,* ‒‧ *key,* ⌣ *no.*

PRECEDING VOWELS

1. ⟍　　⟋　　⟋　　⟋　　⟋　　⟋
　ebb,　aid,　etch,　edge,　off,　oath.

2.  ‒‧　　—　　‧　　⌣　　⌣　　⟋　　⟋
　ache,　egg,　aim,　inn,　own,　awl,　ore.

FOLLOWING VOWELS

3.  ⟋　　⟋　　⟋　　⟋　　⟍　　⎸‧
　low,　row,　woe,　ye,　bow,　day.

4. ⟍　　⟨‧　　—　　—　　⌢　　⌣
　foe,　they,　Kay,　gay,　mow,　knee.

PRECEDING AND FOLLOWING VOWELS

5.  ⟍　　⟋　　⌐　　⟋　　⟋
　ebony,　Italy,　attack,　ashore,　allay.

6.  ⌐　　⟋　　—　　⟋　　⟋
　academy,　arrow,　agony,　afar,　anatomy.

Exercise 5

Read, copy, and transcribe

Write the outline of the word first; then put in the vowel-sign.

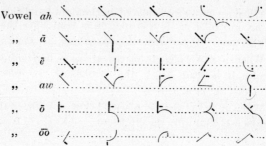

Vowel *ah*

„ *ā*

„ *ē*

„ *aw*

„ *ō*

„ *ōō*

Exercise 6

Read, copy, and transcribe

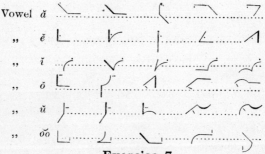

Vowel *ă*

„ *ĕ*

„ *ĭ*

„ *ŏ*

„ *ŭ*

„ *ŏŏ*

Exercise 7

Write in Shorthand

1. Pay, paid, bay, bait, Tay, tame.
2. Say, essay, Esk, escape, low, load.
3. Show, showed, foe, foam, may, make.
4. Weigh, weighed, eight, Etna, nay, name.

Summary

1. There are six long vowels, represented by a heavy dot and dash, and six corresponding short vowels, represented by a light dot and dash.
2. The vowels are called first-place, second-place, and third-place vowels, respectively.
3. The vowel-places are called first, second, and third-places respectively, and vowel-signs are put in the places which correspond with their numbers.
4. Vowel-places are counted from the point at which the stroke begins.
5. Vowel-signs are read as in reading longhand ; (*a*) To downstrokes and upstrokes from left to right ; (*b*) To horizontal strokes from top to bottom, as shown in the following diagrams—

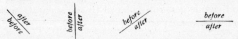

6. In writing a word, the word-form is written first and then the vowel-sign.

CHAPTER III

INTERVENING VOWELS AND POSITION

Intervening Vowels. 21. FIRST- and SECOND-PLACE vowel-signs when occurring between two strokes are written *after the first stroke;* thus, ⌐ *talk,* ⌐ *gate.* THIRD-PLACE vowel-signs are written *before the second stroke* at the end, because the vowel-sign is more conveniently written in that place; thus, ⌐ *deem,* ⌐ *dim,* ⌐ *read,* ⌐ *rid,* ⌐ *pool,* ⌐ *pull.* The vowel-sign is still in the third place, as indicated in the following diagram—

INTERVENING VOWEL PLACES

Compound Words. 22. In compound words the vowel-sign is generally placed to the separate words; as, ⌐ *earache.*

Position of Outlines. 23. Just as there are three places in which to put the vowel-signs, so there are three positions in which to write the outlines of words. The *first* position is *above the line;* the *second* position is *on the line;* and the *third* position is *through the line.* The *first sounded vowel* in the word determines the position of the outline.

When the *first sounded vowel* in a word is a *first-place* vowel, the outline is written in the *first position;* as, ⌐ *palm,* ⌐ *talk,* ⌐ *got,* ⌐ *rod,* ⌐ *wrought.*

When the *first sounded vowel* in a word is a *second-place* vowel, the outline is written in the *second position;* as, ⌐ *bake,* ⌐ *share,* ⌐ *load,* ⌐ *road,* ⌐ *code.*

14

When the *first sounded vowel* in a word is a *third-place* vowel, the outline is written in the *third position* : as, |⸝ *deem*, |⸝ *dim*, ⼂ *lead*, ⼂ *lid*, ⼁ *keyed*, ⼁ *cool*.

24. The first upstroke or downstroke in the outline indicates the position, as shown in the foregoing examples.

It is not practicable to write a horizontal stroke through the line ; therefore, when an outline consists entirely of horizontal strokes, it is written in the *first* position if the first sounded vowel is a first-place vowel, and in the *second* position if the first sounded vowel is either a second- or a third-place vowel ; as, ⌇ *mocking*, ⌇ *making*, ⌇ *meek*, ⌇ *cook*.

Exercise 8

Read and copy

1. *Paul,　Polly,　tall,　Dolly,　bought,　body.*

2. *Coal,　gull,　wrote,　rut,　dome,　dumb.*

3. *Keyed,　kid,　giddy,　leak,　lick,　kill.*

4. *Fade,　fed,　laid,　led,　raid,　red.*

5. *Peel,　pill,　pillow,　pillowed,　bully,　bullied.*

C. *Heed,　hid,　hood,　cheap,　chip,　reap.*

Exercise 9

Read, copy, and transcribe

1.
2.
3.
4.
5.
6.

Exercise 10

Write in Shorthand

1. Patch, batch, Fanny, shop, shoddy, jolly.
2. Paid, page, bake, beck, jail, jelly.
3. Leap, lip, leave, live, lead, lid.
4. Nave, navy, enough, bale, bell, below.
5. May, make, name, namely, comb, money.
6. Feed, food, sheep, ship, loom, limb.

Grammalogues.   25. Frequently-occurring words are represented in shorthand by a single sign, as ＼ for *be*. These words are called *grammalogues* or letter-words, and the shorthand characters that represent them are called *logograms*, or word-letters. At the head of the following Exercises some logograms are given, which must be committed to memory. These characters are written *above*, *on*, or *through* the line, as,

Punctuation.   26. The period, or full stop, is represented by a small cross; thus, ×; the dash thus, ⌐ ; the note of interrogation and the note of exclamation ? and ! respectively. Other punctuation marks are written as usual. Two short lines underneath an outline indicate an initial capital.

GRAMMALOGUES

a, an,   *the ;*   *all,*   *two, too ;*   *of,*   *to ;*

on,   *but ;*   (down) *awe,* *ought,* *aught,*

(down) *who ;*   (up) *and,*   (up) *should.*

Exercise 11
Read, copy, and transcribe

1.

2.

3.

4.

5.

Exercise 12
Write in Shorthand

(THE WORDS PRINTED IN ITALIC TYPE ARE GRAMMALOGUES.)

1. They *should* ask *the* Head *of the* Academy *to* change *the* date.
2. *Who* took *the* padlock off *the* gate *of the* paddock ?

2—(M)

3. Up *to the* date *of the* party she looked both rich *and* happy.
4. *The* head *of the* bank may leave *on* Monday.
5. They *ought to* change *the* date *on the* cheque *to the* fourth *of the* month.

Summary

1. FIRST-PLACE and SECOND-PLACE vowel-signs when occurring between two strokes are written after the first stroke ; THIRD-PLACE vowel-signs are written before the second stroke.
2. The position of an outline is governed by the first sounded vowel in the word.
3. A *grammalogue* is a frequently-occurring *word* represented by a single sign. The *sign* for a grammalogue is called a *logogram*.
4. The full stop is indicated by a small cross, × ; the dash by ⌐⌐ ; mark of interrogation and mark of exclamation by ? and ! respectively.
5. Two short lines underneath an outline indicate an initial capital.

CHAPTER IV

ALTERNATIVE SIGNS FOR *R* AND *H*

Consonant R. 27. The consonant *r* is provided with two different forms in order to facilitate the joining of strokes together, and also for the purpose of indicating an initial or a final vowel sound.

28. Initial *r* is written downward when preceded by a vowel sound ; as, ⁀ *oar*, ⁀ *array*, ⁀ *Arab*.

In other cases, the general rule is to write initial or final *r* upward when it is followed by a vowel sound, and downward when it is not followed by a vowel sound ; as, ⁀ *ray* but ⁀ *air* ; ⁀ *parry* but ⁀ *par* ; ⁀ *tarry* but ⁀ *tar* ; ⁀ *sherry* but ⁀ *share*.

29. Downward *r* is always written initially before *m* because of the easier joining.

Consonant H. 30. The upward form of *h* is most commonly used ; but the downward form is written when the letter stands alone or is immediately followed by ⁀ *k* or ⁀ *g* ; as, ⁀ *hay*, ⁀ *hake*, ⁀ *Haig*.

Exercise 13

Read, copy, and transcribe

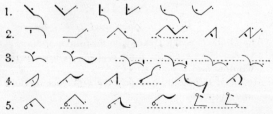

19

Exercise 14

Write in Shorthand

1. Arm, aroma, Orkney, arcade, arrow, ear.
2. Rob, rod, Rodney, Ruth, rage, roach.
3. Perry, Derry, Murray, furrow, morrow, ferry.
4. Deer, jeer, gear, fear, veer, leer.
5. Racy, writ, retail, revere, reverie, wreck.
6. Hook, hog, heath, hatch, hedge, hood.

GRAMMALOGUES

~ *put;* \ *be,* ↘ *to be;* | *it;* ⌐ *had,* | *do,*
⊥ *difference, different;* ⌐ *much,* / *which.*

Exercise 15

Read, copy, and transcribe

1.
2.
3.
4.

5.

Exercise 16

Write in Shorthand

1. They hope *to* reach Orkney *on the* fourth *of* May.
2. *The* red colour *on the* door *and the* yellow *on the* window *had a* poor effect.
3. He *ought to be* fair, *and* pay *the* difference *to* Reid *and* Hannah.

4. If they get *the* money *it should* make *much difference to the* firm.
5. They *had a* heavy mail *on* Monday.
6. Tom saw *the* head *of the* firm leave at four or so.

Summary

1. The consonant *r* initially is written downward if a vowel precedes, and upward if a vowel does not precede.
2. The consonant *r* finally is written upward if a vowel follows, and downward if no vowel follows.
3. Downward *r* is written before *m*.
4. The consonant *h* standing alone, or followed by *k* or *g*, is written downward ; in other cases the upward form is written.

CHAPTER V

DIPHTHONGS

" A diphthong is a union of two vowel sounds in one syllable." (*Prof. Skeat.*)

Diphthongs. 31. There are four common diphthongs, namely, $\bar{i}$, *ow*, *oi*, and $\bar{u}$, as heard in the sentence *I now enjoy music.*

They are represented as follows—

$$\bar{I} \quad OW \quad OI \quad \bar{U}$$

32. The signs for $\bar{i}$ and *oi* are written in the first place; the signs for *ow* and $\bar{u}$ are written in the third place; thus, ⌐ *tie*, ⌐ *time*, ⌐ *toy*, ⌐ *toil*; ⌐ *cow*, ⌐ *cowed*; ⌐ *duty*, ⌐ *mule.*

Joined Diphthongs. 33. The diphthong signs may be joined to the consonant in many words; thus, ⌐ *item*, ⌐ *idle*, ⌐ *ivy*, ⌐ *ice*, ⌐ *eyes*, ⌐ *ire*, ⌐ *isle* or *I'll*, ⌐ *I'm (I am)*, ⌐ *nigh*, ⌐ *now*, ⌐ *bow*, ⌐ *avow*, ⌐ *dew*, ⌐ *Matthew*, ⌐ *issue*, ⌐ *owl.*

34. The semicircle representing $\bar{u}$ may be written ⌐ for convenience in joining; thus, ⌐ *cue*, ⌐ *argue*, ⌐ *mew*, ⌐ *new*, ⌐ *value.* The sign for $\bar{i}$ is abbreviated when prefixed to *l* and *m*, and the sign for *ow* is abbreviated when affixed to *n*, as shown in the examples in paragraph 33.

Triphones. 35. A small tick attached to a diphthong-sign represents any vowel immediately following the diphthong; thus, ⌐ *diary*, ⌐ *loyal*,

22

vowel, *attenuate,* *annual,* *annuity,* *riot,* *ingenuous.*

These signs are called *triphones* because they represent three vowels in one sign.

Abbreviated W. 36. The initial sound of *w*, before *k, g, m, r* is represented by a right semicircle; thus, *wake,* *wig,* *womanly,* *wear,* *wary.*

37. When *w* is preceded by a vowel, the stroke must be written; as, *awake,* *awoke,* *aware.*

Exercise 17
Read, copy, and transcribe

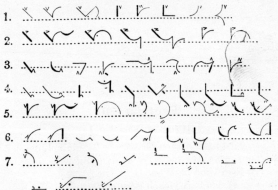

Exercise 18
Write in Shorthand

1. Bite, tile, time, timely, ripe, ride, fire, fiery.
2. Coil, coiling, toyed, joy, enjoy, coinage, Doyle.
3. Rout, rowdy, cowed, pouch, vouch, loud.

4. View, review, dupe, tunic, fury, mule.
5. Item, eyes, nigh, deny, voyage, argue, arguing, genuine.
6. Wear, wary, weary, woke, awoke, war, warm.

GRAMMALOGUES

∧ *how,* ⌐ *why;* ⌐ *beyond,* ∩ *you;* / *large;* — *can,*

— *come;* — *go,* — *give-n;* ⌐ *for;* ⌐ *have.*

Exercise 19

Read, copy, and transcribe

Exercise 20

Write in Shorthand

1. *How can you* attach *the* wire *to the* high chimney ?
2. They were due *to* arrive at five, *but* were delayed *a* long time at Wick.
3. *You should* verify each item *on the* bill.
4. *Do you* like *the* new tyre *you have had put on the* car ?
5. Few *of the* party knew *why you had to go to* Newquay *on the* tenth *of* July.
6. *A* week ago I saw Doyle, *but he had* no time *to give to* my work ; *he had to* hurry *for the* boat.

Summary

1. The four diphthongs are *ī, ow, oi, ū*.
2. The diphthongs *ī* and *oi* are put in the *first* vowel-place ; and *ow* and *ū* in the *third* vowel-place.
3. A diphthong may be joined to a stroke where convenient.
4. A small tick attached to a diphthong sign indicates the addition of a vowel to the diphthong.
5. Initial *w* before *k, g, m, r,* is represented by a right semicircle.

CHAPTER VI

PHRASEOGRAPHY

Phrasing. 38. Phraseography is the writing of two or more words together without lifting the pen, the resulting outline being called a *phraseogram*. The best phraseograms are those which combine the qualities of *facility*, *lineality*, and *legibility*. A phraseogram should be easy to write ; it should not ascend too far above, nor descend too far below, the line ; and it must be legible when written. Subject to the observance of these conditions, the practice of phrase writing will greatly increase the writer's fluency and speed.

(*a*) The first word-form of a phraseogram must occupy the position in which it would be written if it stood alone. Thus, the phrase *How can they* would be represented by the outline ⌒⟨ , commencing *on* the line, because *how*, if it stood alone, would be written on the line. Similarly, ⟍ *I have* commences *above* the line, because *I*, standing alone, would be written above the line.

(*b*) A first-position word-form may be slightly raised or lowered, however, to permit of a following stroke being written *above*, *on* or *through* the line ; as, ⟍ *I thank you* (and using the logogram ⌣ *with*), ⟋ *with much*, ⟋ *with which*, ⟍ *with each.*

(c) When joined to *k*, *m*, *l* (up), the sign ⌄⁀ *may* be shortened ; thus, ⁀ *I can,* ⁀ *I am,* ⌁ *I will.*

(d) With rare exceptions it is unnecessary to vocalize phraseograms. The word *he* standing alone, or at the beginning of a phrase, is written ⌁ ; but in the middle of a phrase the word is represented by the logogram ı ; thus, ⌁ *he may,* ⌁ *if he may,* ⌁ *he should know,* ⌁ *if he should know.* For the sake of an easier joining the word *much* is some- times written in full in phrases ; as, ⌁ *so much,* ⌁ *how much ;* and *were* is written either ⁄ or ⌁ ; thus, ⌁ *they were,* ⌁ *you were,* ⌁ *we were,* ⌁ *if he were.* In phrases, the word *him* should have the dot vowel inserted ; thus, ⌁ *of him,* ⌁ *to him.*

Tick *the*. 39. The word *the* may be expressed by a light slanting *tick*, joined to a preceding character and written either downward (from right to left) or upward (from left to right).

(a) DOWNWARD : ⌁ *of the,* ⌁ *and the,* ⌁ *should the,* ⌁ *with the,* ⌁ *by the,* ⌁ *if the,* ⌁ *have the.*

(b) UPWARD : ⌁ *beyond the,* ⌁ *what the,* ⌁ *how the,* ⌁ *at the,* ⌁ *which the,* ⌁ *was the.*

This tick for *the* must never be used initially.

NOTE— ⌁ *on the* and ⌁ *but the* should slope a little to secure a better angle.

PHRASES

I thank you		why have you
I think you should be		with you
I have the		so much
I have had		with much
I saw the		with which
I see		with each
I am		when they
I may be		what do you
I will		what was
I will be		what can be
you should		it would be
you should be		it should be
you can		it will be
you will		it was
you will be		which was
you may be		which were
you were		he should be
if you were		he will be
they were		if he
how can they		if he were
why do you		too much

Grammalogues

thank-ed, *think*; *though*, *them*; *was*, *whose*; *shall*, *wish*; *with*, *when*; *what*, *would*; *O, oh, owe*, *he*.

Exercise 21

Read, copy, and transcribe

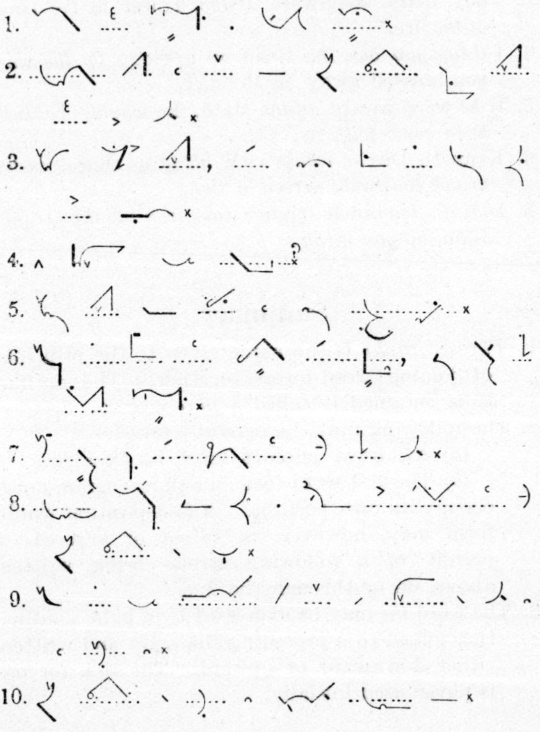

Exercise 22

Write in Shorthand

(Phraseograms in the following letterpress exercises are indicated by the hyphen.)

1. *Why-do-you* think he-*was* aware *of-the* likely failure *of-the* firm ?

2. I-*thank-you for-the* tube *of* colour, *which* I-*think should-be all*-right.

3. They deny they-were at-*the* Tower at-*the* time *of-the* fire.

4. I-*think-you* owe *the* Head *an* apology *for-the* way *you* hurried away *on*-Monday.

5. If-*he*-were aware *of-the* date, he-*would*, I-*think*, *have come with* us.

6. Kenneth Doyle, *whose* view *all of* us share, wrote *to* say he-*would* arrive at five.

7. I-*think too*-much time *was-given to-the* topic. *What-do-you think ?*

Summary

1. *Phraseography* is the name given to the principle of joining word-forms together. The outline thus obtained is called a *phraseogram*.

2. The following must be carefully noted—

   (*a*) Awkward joinings must be avoided.

   (*b*) The first word-form in a phraseogram must occupy its own position. A first-position word-form may, however, be raised or lowered to permit of a following stroke being written above, on or through the line.

3. The word *the* may be expressed by a light slanting tick joined to a preceding character and written either downward or upward. The tick for *the* is never used initially.

CHAPTER VII

CIRCLE *S* AND *Z*

Circle S and Z.   40. The consonants *S* and *Z* are represented not only by the strokes) and) but also by a small circle o   Initially the circle represents the light sound of *s* only ; medially and finally it represents the sound of *s* or *z*.   The sound of *z* initially must be represented by the stroke) as, ⟋ *zeal,* ⟍ *zero,* ⟍ *zenith.*

Left and Right Motion.   41. In this chapter, and in the following pages, the term *Left Motion* means the motion of the hand in writing the longhand letter ⟲ ⟳, the opposite motion being termed the *Right Motion* ⟲.   The circle *s*, when standing alone, is written with the *left* motion.

42. The circle *s* is written (*a*) inside curves, (*b*) outside angles, and (*c*) with the *left* motion when joined to straight strokes not forming an angle ; thus,

(*a*) ⟍ *safes,* ⟍ *soothes,* ⟋ *essays,* ⟍ *sashes,* ⟍ *seems,* ⟍ *sense,* ⟍ *sings,* ⟍ *slays,* ⟍ *source,* ⟍ *fossil,* ⟍ *thistle,* ⟍ *Cecil,* ⟍ *muscle,* ⟍ *nestles,* ⟍ *designs,* ⟍ *lisps.*

(*b*) ⟍ *gasp,* ⟍ *rasp,* ⟍ *risk,* ⟍ *task,* ⟍ *Biscay,* ⟍ *justice,* ⟍ *hasp.*

(*c*) ⟍ *space,* ⟍ *seeds,* ⟍ *sages,* ⟍ *soaks,* ⟍ *sorrows,* ⟍ *Busby,* ⟍ *tacit,* ⟍ *cask,* ⟍ *razor,* ⟍ *wiser.*

31

43. Initial circle *s* is always read *first;* final circle *s* is always read *last;* and vowel signs are placed and read in relation to the stroke consonant, and not to the circle, as in the foregoing examples.

44. The circle *s* may be added to a stroke logogram, as, ___ *come,* ___*o comes,* ___ *put,* ___ *puts.*

Stroke L and Circle. 45. When the stroke *l* immediately precedes or follows a circle which is attached to a curve, it is written in the same direction as the circle; thus, ___ *lesson,* ___ *cancel,* ___ *vessel,* ___ *loser.*

46. A lightly-sounded vowel may be omitted, as in ___ *poison,* ___ *refusal,* ___ *answer,* ___ *desire.*

Exercise 23

Read, copy, and transcribe

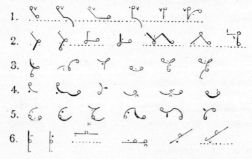

Exercise 24

Write in Shorthand

1. Lays, slays, oars, soars, face, facing.
2. Poison, poisonous, pacifies, voicing, rising, toilsome.
3. Dusky, excites, customs, justice, rusty, suffice.
4. Less, Leslie, shame, shameless, shamelessly, slums.
5. Excusing, refusing, spacing, basin, dozen, resigns.
6. Hope, hopeless, hopelessly, consul, pencil, fossils.

GRAMMALOGUES

usual-ly; *as, has,* *is, his;* *because;* *itself;* *those, thyse'f,* *this,* *thus.*

Exercise 25

Read, copy, and transcribe

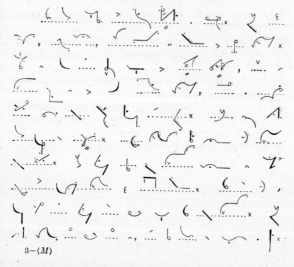

Exercise 26

Write in Shorthand

If Miss Nelson *wishes to* see-*the* works, she *can come to-this* office *on* Tuesday or Wednesday *of-this* week, *and-*I-*shall-be* happy *to* show *all-the* details she may desire *to* see.   I-*think-it-is but* fair *to* say *this is-the* busy season *with* us, *and* I-*shall-have but a* few minutes *to* spare *to* Miss Nelson.   My deputy *can* take charge *of-the* lady.   I-will *thank-you* if-*you-*will *put-the* facts *to-the* lady *as* nicely *as you-can, because* she may *think* I-am *an* idle fellow *with-much* time at-my disposal.   I-know *you-*will excuse *this* appeal, *and-*I hope *you-*will-*do what* I ask, *as* I *should-be* sorry *to* upset Miss Nelson, or *to* appear *to be* rude *when* she *comes.*

Summary

1. A small circle used initially represents *s* only ; medially and finally it represents *s* or *z*.
2. The circle *s* is written outside angles, inside curves, and with the left motion to straight strokes not forming an angle.
3. An *initial* circle is always read *first ;* a *final* circle is always read *last.*
4. The stroke *l*, immediately preceding or following a circle attached to a curve, is written in the same direction as the circle.
5. The circle *s* may be added to stroke logograms.

CHAPTER VIII

STROKE *S* AND *Z*

Stroke S and Z. 47. Wherever there is an initial
or a final vowel *sound*, there must be a stroke consonant, to provide a place for the vowel *sign*. Therefore, the stroke *s* must be written when a vowel
precedes initial *s*, or when a vowel follows final *s* or *z*;
thus, ⟩ *ace,* ⟩ *say;* ⟍ *oose,* ⟍ *zoo;* ⟍ *asp,* but
⟍ *sap;* ⟍ *ask,* but ⟍ *sack;* ⟍ *racy,* but
⟍ *race;* ⟍ *busy,* but ⟍ *bees.*

48. Where the stroke *s* is written initially in the
root word, it is retained in compounds and in
derivatives formed by means of a prefix, thus,
⟍ *saw,* ⟍ *saw-bench,* ⟍ *assailed,* ⟍ *unassailed,*
⟍ *ease,* ⟍ *disease.*

The stroke is also written—

(*a*) In words like ⟍ *science,* ⟍ *sewer,* where a
triphone immediately follows initial *s*.

(*b*) In words like ⟍ *cease,* ⟍ *saucer,* where initial
s is immediately followed by a vowel and another
s or *z*.

(*c*) In words like ⟍ *sinuous,* ⟍ *tortuous,*
⟍ *joyous,* where the final syllable -*ous* is immediately preceded by a diphthong.

Exercise 27

Read, copy, and transcribe

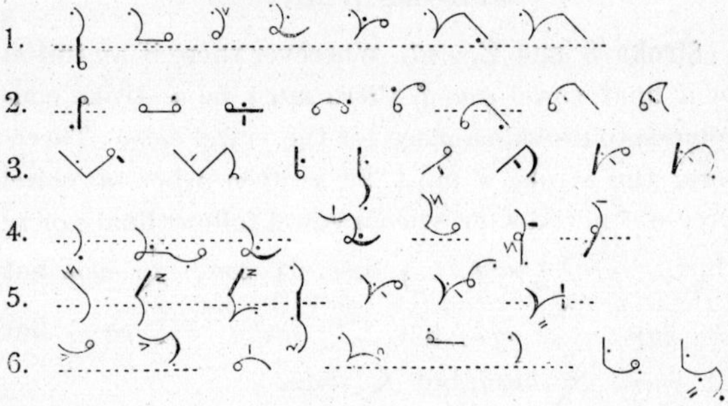

Exercise 28

Write in Shorthand

1. Asp, aside, assess, Assam, assailing, asylum, assayed.
2. Base, basso, juice, juicy, legs, legacy, coals, colza.
3. Spouse, espouse, seek, Essex, score, Oscar, Isaac.
4. Essays, essence, escapes, Eskimo, say, aces.
5. Siamese, sciatica, sighing, easy, uneasy, uneasily, uneasiness.
6. Sinuous, tortuous, vacuous, tenuous, ingenuous.

GRAMMALOGUES

me, *him*: *myself*, *himself*; *special-ly*,

speak; *subject-ed*: *several*.

Exercise 29

Read, copy, and transcribe

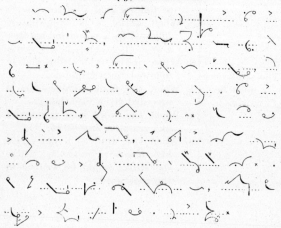

Exercise 30

Write in Shorthand

For several special reasons I *should* like *you to-come and* see *me on* Wednesday *as* early *as you-can.* I *specially* desire *you to-*write out-*the* names *of all-the* firms *with-which-you have-had* business dealings since *you* came *to* us. I-*shall* discuss *a* new policy *with-you, and-the* names *for-which* I ask may-*be of* use. I-*am a* bit upset at-*the* refusal *of* Askew *and* Benson *to-*take *those* Eskimo rugs, *and-*I *should* like *to* know-*the* reasons *for-the* refusal. I-*have several subjects* besides these *of-which* I-*wish to speak to-you* when I-*see-you* on Wednesday. Ask *to* see *me as* soon *as you* arrive.

Summary

The stroke *s* or *z* must be written :

1. When a vowel precedes initial *s* or follows final *s* or *z*.
2. When initial *s* is immediately followed by a vowel and another *s* or *z*.
3. When initial *s* is immediately followed by a triphone.
4. When the final syllable *-ous* is preceded by a diphthong.
5. When the word is a compound like *sea-mew, saw-bench*.
6. When the word is a derivative like *unceasing, unassailed*, where the stroke would be written in the root word.

CHAPTER IX

LARGE CIRCLES *SW* AND *SS* OR *SZ*

SW Circle. 49. A large INITIAL circle, written with the same motion as the circle *s*, represents the double consonant *sw*, thus, ⎧ *seat*, ⎧ *sweet*, ⌐ *sum*, ⌐ *swum*. As a vowel cannot be written to a circle, the stroke *w* must be written in words like ⌐ *sway*, ⌐ *suasive*. The *sw* circle is used initially only.

SS Circle. 50. A large MEDIAL or FINAL circle, written with the same motion as circle *s*, represents *s-s*, having a light or heavy sound, with the intervening vowel *ĕ*; thus, ⎧ (*ses*) *necessily* ; ⎧ (*sez*) *passes* ; ⎧ (*zes*) *possessive* ; ⎧ (*zez*) *causes*. When a vowel other than *ĕ* intervenes, it is indicated by placing the vowel-sign within the circle ; thus, ⎧ *exist*, ⎧ *exhaust*, ⎧ *exercised*. Final *s* is added thus, ⎧ *exercises*. The large circle is also used to express the sounds of two *s*'s in consecutive syllables, as in ⎧ *mis-spell*.

Plurals and Possessives. 51. As ⎧ *Lucy*, ⎧ *policy*, ⎧ *jealousy*, etc., are written with the stroke *s*, the stroke *s* is retained in the derived words ⎧ *Lucy's*, ⎧ *policies*, ⎧ *jealousies*. (See also pars. 47 and 48.)

52. A few words ending in *s-s* are written with the circle and stroke, or the stroke and circle, in order to distinguish them from other words containing similar consonants, and in which the large

circle is employed ; thus, ⟩ *possess*, but ⟜ *pauses* ;

⟩ *access*, but ⟝ *axis* ; ⟩ *recess*, but ⟩ *races*.

Large Circles in Phraseography. 53. The *sw* circle is used for the words *as we* in phrases like ⟨ *as we have*, ⟜ *as we can*, and for *as w-* in 𝟞 *as well as ;* and the *ss* circle for the two *s*'s in phrases like ⟨ *in this city*, ⟨ *this is*, ⟝ *as is*, or *as has*,

○ *is as* or *is his*.

Exercise 31

Read, copy, and transcribe

1. ⟜ ⟝ ⟝ ⟝ ⟝ ⟝ ⟝

2. ⟍ ⟍ ⟝ ⟝ ⟝ ⟝ ⟝

3. ⟍ ⟍ ⟝ ⟝ ⟝ ⟝

4. ⟍ ⟍ ⟝ ⟝ ⟝ ⟝ ⟝

5. ⟝ ⟝ ⟝ ⟝ ⟝ ⟝ ⟝

6. ⟝ ⟝ ⟝ ⟝ ⟝ ⟝ ⟝ ⟝

7. ⟝ ⟝ ⟝ ⟝ ⟝ ⟝ ⟝

Exercise 32

Write in Shorthand

1. Sweetly, sweetness, swig, swain, swing, swimmer.
2. Entices, reduces, revises, ounces, minces, laces.
3. Roses, peruses, terraces, essences, fences, romances.
4. Dazes, decisive, races, resist, misses, Mississippi.
5. Fallacy, fallacies, Morrissey, Morrissey's, curacy, curacies.
6. Thesis, emphasis, paralysis, Genesis, Nemesis, axis.

GRAMMALOGUES

in, any,   own ;   your,   year ;   are,
our, hour :   ourselves,   themselves.

Exercise 33

Read, copy, and transcribe

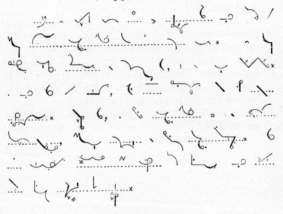

Exercise 34

Write in Shorthand

The invoices *and* bills *of* lading *for-the* valances *and* laces *are* ready *for* despatch, *and-the* cases *themselves are to-*leave *by-the* " Swiss Valley," sailing *on* Wednesday. *The* advices *should-be with our* customers *by-the* tenth *of-*March, *and-*they-will-*do all-*they *can to-*make *a* success *of-the* deal. They know-*the* business thoroughly, *and you-*may safely leave *it to-them. It-is* scarcely necessary *to* emphasize *what* they *themselves* know *al*ready.

Summary

1. A large initial circle represents *sw*.
2. A large medial or final circle represents the light or heavy sound of *s-s* with an intervening vowel.
3. Where a root word ends with stroke *s*, the plural, possessive, or third person singular is formed by the addition of the circle *s*.
4. Where a root word ends with a circle *s*, the plural, possessive, or the third person singular is formed by the use of the large circle *ses*.
5. A few words ending in *s-s* are written with the circle and stroke, or with the stroke and circle, to distinguish them from words in which the large circle is employed.
6. The *sw* circle is used in phrases like *as well as, as we know ;* and the *ss* circle in phrases like *it is said, in this city.*

CHAPTER X

LOOP *ST* AND *STR*

Loop ST. 54. The combination *st*, as in *st*eam, mi*st*, pa*ssed* (pa*st*) is represented by a loop made half the length of the stroke to which it is attached ; thus, ⌒ *scem*, ⌒ *steam*, ∿ *sown*, ∿ *stone*, ⌒ *sake*, ⌒ *stake*, ⌒ *miss*, ⌒ *mist*, ⌒ *lace*, ⌒ *laced*, ⌒ *pass*, ⌒ *past*.

Like the circle *s*, the *st* loop is written with the Left motion to straight strokes and inside curves, as shown above. Like the circle *s*, too, the *st* loop is always read first at the beginning of the stroke and last at the end.

55. Since a final *vowel* sound requires a final *stroke*, in order to provide a place for the vowel-sign (par. 47), it follows that the *st* loop cannot be employed finally when a vowel follows *t ;* thus, ⌉ *best*, but ⌉ *bestow ;* ∠ *rust*, but ∠ *rusty ;* ⌐ *honest*, but ⌐ *honesty.*

56. The *st* loop may also be employed finally for the heavy sound of *zd*, as in the words ⌐ *fused*, ⌐ *refused*, ⌐ *opposed*, ⌐ *disposed.* The word *caused* is written ⌐ to distinguish it from ⌐ *cost.*

Loop STR. 57. A large loop, extending two-thirds of the length of the stroke to which it is attached, represents *str*. This *str* (ster) loop *is never written at the beginning of an outline.* Like the circle *s* and the *st* loop, the *str* loop is written with the Left

43

motion to straight strokes, and inside curves; thus, ⟋ *pass,* ⟍ *past,* ⟍ *pastor,* ⟋ *fast,* ⟍ *faster.*

58. The *st* and *str* loops may be used medial!y where a good joining results; thus, ⟋ *justify,* ⟋ *elastic,* ⟍ *masterpiece.*

59. The *st* loop cannot be employed when a vowel occurs between *s* and *t,* nor can the *str* loop be written when a strongly sounded vowel occurs between *st* and *r,* because where there is a vowel sound there must be a stroke consonant to provide a place for the vowel-sign (par. 47). Compare ⟍ *best* and ⟍ *beset,* ⟋ *rest* and ⟋ *receipt,* ⟍ *pastor,* ⟍ *pasture,* ⟍ *poster,* ⟍ *posture.*

60. The circle *s* is added to a final loop as follows— ⟋ *taste,* ⟋ *tastes;* ⟋ *lustre,* ⟋ *lustres.*

Exercise 35

Read, copy, and transcribe

1.

2.

3.

4.

5.

6.

7.

Exercise 36

Write in Shorthand

1. Stout, stoutly, stock, stockade, style, stylish.
2. Rust, rusts, nest, nests, waste, wastes.
3. Box, boxed, lapse, lapsed, refuse, refused.
4. Coaster, coasters, boaster, boasters, muster.
5. Stone, stole, stave, stem, stung, star.
6. Gassed, gazette, vest, visit, rust, russet.
7. Bolsters, barrister, waster, lustre, sinister, minister.

GRAMMALOGUES

*first. influence, influenced. next.
most, language, owing, thing, young,
Lord, we.*

Exercise 37

Read, copy, and transcribe

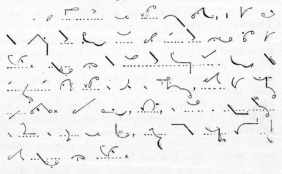

Exercise 38

Write in Shorthand

The *language* of-*the young* barrister *in-the* case *was* *most* stately, *and* it-*must* *have influenced* both judge *and* jury. *It* almost looked *as-if-the* case *was* lost *at-the first*, *because* of-*the* calm way *in-which-the* opposing counsel set out *to* state-*the* facts *for-his* side. *But-the young* barrister faced *the* test fairly, *and-his* *language* and style, *though different*, showed *him to* be *a* master of-*law and* logic. *We-shall* watch *his* career *at-the* bar, *and-we-think* he-*must* succeed *because* of-*his* abilities.

Revisionary Exercise (A)

Write in Shorthand

If-you-can put me up *for a* week *in* August, I-*shall-* be ready *to-go and* stay *with-you*. *You-can-have* as *much* walking *as you*-like. I-*shall-be* at-*your* disposal at *almost any hour*, *and-as* I-*am a* rare walker *myself*, I-*think* I-*can* say *you*-will-*have* all-*the* exercise *you* wish. *You* ought-*to* be *a different* fellow *when* I-leave, *if-you-will-be influenced* by-*me*. I-*think* I-*can give-you a* mile *in* six *and* beat *you*. I-*have-had* some talk *with young* Lord Robson *several*-times *in-the* past week, *and* he says *you-can-do* five miles *an* hour. *Those-who* saw *you* last autumn *and*-know *what you-can-do*, all say-*the* same *thing*. *This-is* *all* I-know *as to-your* form. *But-we-shall*-see *for* ourselves. I-*think-you*-will *own* I-*am* far *beyond you* *in* speed. *It*-will-*be a* case of-each *for-himself and-* *the* race *to-the* faster of-*the* two. *Oh*, I-know I-*shall* beat *you*, unless *you-are* faster *this year*. *Those-* *who think* poorly of-*themselves* only induce *those-*

who know *them to-think-the* same. I *speak for-myself, because* I-know *myself.* I-*can* say *a* deal *on-this subject, and-*I *usually do-*so. *You* ask *why* I-*have* stayed away so-long. *The* answer *is* business keeps *me* away. *When would-you* like *me to-come ? The* best *of* luck *to-you and to-the* rest *of-the* family ! *It-*will-*be* nice *to* see *them* all, *though* I-saw *most of-them a* month or-*two* ago.   (283 words)

Summary

1. A small loop represents *st* ; a large loop represents *str*.

2. The *st* loop may be used initially, medially or finally.

3. The *st* loop may be employed finally to represent the sound of *zd*.

4. The *str* loop may be used medially or finally, but not initially.

5. The *st* loop cannot be employed when a vowel occurs between *s* and *t*, nor can the loop be written immediately before a final vowel.

6. The *str* loop cannot be written when a strongly sounded vowel occurs between *st* and *r*.

CHAPTER XI

INITIAL HOOKS TO STRAIGHT STROKES AND CURVES

Double Consonants. 61. The liquids *r* and *l* frequently blend with other consonants so as to form a double consonant, as in the words *pr*ay, *bl*ow, *dr*ink, *gl*are, *fr*y, *fl*y, or are separated from a preceding consonant by an obscure vowel only, as in pa*per*, ma*ker*, ta*ble*, ba*bel*. These consonant combinations are represented by prefixing a hook to the simple shorthand characters to indicate their union with *r* and *l*.

R Hook to Straight Strokes. 62. A small initial hook, written with the Right motion, adds *R* to straight strokes ; thus,

$$\diagdown \quad \diagdown \quad \diagdown \quad \uparrow \quad \uparrow \quad \nearrow \quad \nearrow \quad \leftarrow \quad \leftarrow$$

p,   *pr,*   *br,*   *tr,*   *dr,*   *chr,*   *jr,*   *kr,*   *gr.*

L Hook to Straight Strokes. 63. A small initial hook, written with the Left motion, adds *L* to straight strokes ; thus,

$$\diagdown \quad \diagdown \quad \diagdown \quad \uparrow \quad \uparrow \quad \nearrow \quad \nearrow \quad \leftarrow \quad \leftarrow$$

p,   *pl,*   *bl,*   *tl,*   *dl,*   *chl,*   *jl,*   *kl,*   *gl.*

R Hook to Curved Strokes. 64. A *small* initial hook, written inside the curve, adds *r* to a curved stroke ; thus,

$$\diagdown \quad \diagdown \quad \diagdown \quad \diagdown \quad \diagdown \quad \diagdown \quad \diagdown \quad \frown \quad \smile$$

f,   *fr,*   *vr,*   *thr,*   *THr,*   *shr,*   *zhr,*   *mr,*   *nr.*

L Hook to Curved Strokes. 65. A *large* initial hook, written inside the curve, adds *l* to a curved stroke ; thus,

$$\smile \quad \subset \quad \subset \quad (\quad \cup \text{(upward)} \quad \frown \quad \smile$$

 f, *fl,* *vl,* *thl,* *shl,*   *ml,* *nl.*

66. The stroke ╱ *r* is not hooked initially, because the characters ╱ and ╱ are employed for *w* and *y.*

SHR and SHL. 67. The double consonant ╮ *shr* is always written *downward*, and the double consonant ╰ *shl* is always written *upward.*

Small Hook to NG. 68. The hooked form ╰ represents *ng-kr* or *ng-gr*, as heard in the words ban*ker*, fin*ger*.

69. The hooked forms should be called by their syllabic names ; as, ╲ *per*, ╲ *pel*, ╰ *fer*, ╰ *fel*, etc.

Vowels and Double Consonants. 70. Vowels are placed and read to the hooked forms as they are placed and read to the simple forms ; thus, ╲ *pie*, ╲ *ply*, ╲ *apply ;* ╱ *lead*, ╱ *leader*, ╱ *leaderless ;* ╲ *pity*, ╲ *pretty ;* ╲ *Peter*, ╲ *Peterloo ;* ╽ *tie*, ╽ *try*, ╽ *trifle*, ╽ *trifler.*

Extended Use of L Hook. 71. In order to obtain easier forms the *l* hook is sometimes used in words in which the *l* properly belongs to the following syllable, and not to the stroke to which it is attached ; thus, ╽ *deeply*, ╲ *briefly*, ╲ *briefless*, ╭ *thinly*, ╰ *enlivener*, ╲ *peevishly.*

Exercise 39

Read, copy, and transcribe

1. [shorthand outlines]
2. [shorthand outlines]
3. [shorthand outlines]
4. [shorthand outlines]
5. [shorthand outlines]
6. [shorthand outlines]
7. [shorthand outlines]

Exercise 40

Write in Shorthand

1. Pry, pride, preach, preacher, bray, break, breaker.
2. Crow, croak, cricket, grew, group, grape, bigger.
3. Ply, plied, played, plum, place, replace, replaces.
4. Problem, enclose, enclosure, blow, blows, bluster.
5. Double, pedal, fiddle, model, fickle, glow, gloat.
6. Fred, afraid, tougher, other, otherwise, every, usher, pressure, inner.
7. Honour, honourable, flavour, flower, Fletcher, faithful, privilege, Marshall, specialize.

GRAMMALOGUES

principle, principal-ly; *liberty,* *member, remember-ed,* *number-ed;* *truth;* *Dr., doctor,* *dear,* *during;* *chair,* *cheer; larger;* *care.*

Exercise 41

Read, copy, and transcribe

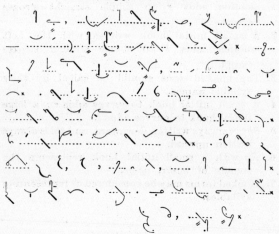

Exercise 42

Write in Shorthand

Dear-Sir,

Thank-you for-your favour of-the first of April, and-for mailing me your price-lists and samples of blue and black inks and glue in-the several sizes of bottles. I-think-the labels are better and brighter now. I-shall give-the samples a fair trial during-the next few weeks, and, if suitable, I-may-be able to stock a large number of-the smaller sizes. As I-think-you know, my principal business is with legal offices, and, as you-will agree, it-is essential to offer them only first-class inks.

Yours-truly,

Summary

1. A small initial hook written with the Right motion adds *r* to simple straight strokes except ╱

2. A small initial hook written with the Left motion adds *l* to simple straight strokes except ╱

3. The hooked signs should be called by their syllabic names.

4. A small initial hook to curves adds *r* ; a large initial hook to curves adds *l*.

5. *Shr* is always written downward, and *shl* is always written upward.

6. *Ng* with a small initial hook represents the sounds of *ng-kr*, *ng-gr*.

7. Hooked forms may be considered as representing syllables.

CHAPTER XII

ALTERNATIVE FORMS

Additional Signs for FR, VR, etc. 72. The strokes
〵 *r,* 〳 *s,* are not hooked for the addition of
r or *l*. They are, however, hooked to provide
alternative forms for *fr, vr, fl, vl, thr,* THr; thus,

fr,	*vr,*	*thr,*	THr,	*fl,*	*vl.*

The first form of each pair is called a *left* curve,
because it is made with the Left motion ; the second
form of each pair is called a *right* curve, because it
is made with the Right motion. There is only one
form for *thl* (, namely, the left curve.

73. (*a*) When standing alone, the *left* curves for
fr, vr, thr, are used if a vowel precedes, and the
right curves if a vowel does not precede ; thus,
affray, fray, ether, three.

(*b*) When joined to another stroke, the form is
used which gives the easier joining, preference
being given to the right forms ; thus, Friday,
virtue, frame, verbal, thermal,
leather, coffer, lover. Generally, it will
be found that the *left* curves join better with strokes
written towards the *left*, and the *right* curves with
strokes written towards the *right*.

FL and VL. 74. The right curves 〵 *fl,* 〵 *vl* are
used only after *straight upstrokes* and the *horizontals*
— *k,* — *g,* ⌣ *n ;* thus, cavil, naval,

53

↘ *rifle*, ↘ *weevil*. In all other cases the left curves ⌣ *fl*, ⌣ *vl* are used ; thus, ⌣ *flow*, ⌣ *aflow*, ⌣ *flake*, ⌣ *flicker*, ⌣ *joyful*, ↘ *arrival*.

Intervening Vowels. 75. (*a*) In order to obtain a briefer or an easier outline, an initially hooked form may be used even when a vowel separates *l* or *r* from the stroke consonant. Where necessary, an intervening dot vowel between a stroke and an initial hook may be indicated by writing a small circle, instead of a dot, either after or before the stroke ; thus, ↘ *barley*, ↙ *challenge*, ⌐ *narrate*, ↙ *sharply* ; and an intervening dash vowel or diphthong may be indicated by striking the sign through the stroke consonant ; thus, ↘ *Burmah*, ⌐ *coarsely*, ↗ *nullify*, ⌐ *lecture*.

(*b*) If the vowel-sign cannot easily be written through the stroke, it may be placed at the beginning or the end for a first-place or a third-place vowel respectively ; thus, ⌐ *corner*, ↘ *tolerable*, ⌐ *captures*.

(*c*) In words like ↘ *perceive*, ⌐ *telegraphy*, ↗ *mercury*, ↘ *nervously*, the hooked form sufficiently represents the first syllable of the word. With the exception of ↘ *nurse*, ⌐ *Turk*, ⌐ *dark*, and a few other words, the initially hooked strokes are not used in monosyllables where the consonants are separated by a vowel. Such words as ↘ *pair*,

╲╱ *pale,* ╘ *tare,* ╘ *tore* are written with the separate strokes, so as to indicate the intervening vowel.

Exercise 43

Read, copy, and transcribe

1. ░░░░░░░░░░░░░░░░░░░░░░░░░░░░░░░░░░░░

2. ░░░░░░░░░░░░░░░░░░░░░░░░░░░░░░░░░░░░

3. ░░░░░░░░░░░░░░░░░░░░░░░░░░░░░░░░░░░░

4. ░░░░░░░░░░░░░░░░░░░░░░░░░░░░░░░░░░░░

5. ░░░░░░░░░░░░░░░░░░░░░░░░░░░░░░░░░░░░

6. ░░░░░░░░░░░░░░░░░░░░░░░░░░░░░░░░░░░░

7. ░░░░░░░░░░░░░░░░░░░░░░░░░░░░░░░░░░░░

8. ░░░░░░░░░░░░░░░░░░░░░░░░░░░░░░░░░░░░

Exercise 44

Write in Shorthand

1. Fray, three, Friday, frank, differ, endeavour.
2. Free, freely, thrifty, recover, waver, Waverley.
3. Flood, flask, flock, playful, grateful, effectively.
4. Baffle, trifle, shovel, removal, inflame.
5. Rival, roughly, hovel, cavalry, gravel.
6. Charming, courage, encourage, furnace, Norwich.

GRAMMALOGUES

╲ *people ;* ╲ *belief, believe-d ;* │ *tell,* ╶│ *till ;*

│ *deliver-ed-y ;* ╱ *largely ;* ── *call,* ⌐ *equal-ly ;*

╰ *over,* ╰ *however ;* ╰ *valuation.*

Exercise 45

Read, copy, and transcribe

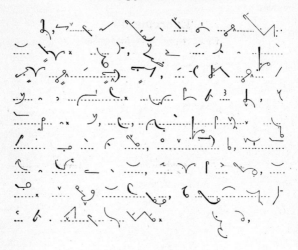

Exercise 46

Write in Shorthand

Have-you ever noticed *what* useful lessons *you-may*-receive through *a* shrewd look at-*the* faces *of-the people you-come* across *in* travelling? *You*-will-see *in-them* humour *and* gloom; generosity *and* miserable stinginess; pluck *and* nervous fear; wisdom *and* simplicity. *You*-will-notice *the* drinker *and-the* abstainer; *the* hopeful *and-the* fearful; *the* clever talker *and-the* bore; *the* flighty *and-the* modest; *the* pilferer *and-the* honest fellow; *the* loafer *and-the* worker. Five minutes *in* a tramway car may offer us many lessons if-*we care to*-take *them*.

Summary

1. (*a*) When standing alone, the left curves $\smallsmile$ *fr*,
      $\smallsmile$ *vr*, $($ *thr*, $($ THr are used if a vowel
      precedes, and the right curves $\searrow$ *fr*, $\searrow$ *vr*,
      $)$ *thr*, $)$ THr, if a vowel does not precede.
   (*b*) When joined to another stroke either curve is
      used in order to secure an easier joining.

2. The right curves $\searrow$ *fl*, $\searrow$ *vl* are used after
   straight upstrokes, and after the horizontals
   $\underline{\quad}$ *k*, $\underline{\quad}$ *g*, and $\smallsmile$ *n*; in all other cases the
   left curves $\smallsmile$ *fl*, $\smallsmile$ *vl* are used.

3. (*a*) An intervening dot vowel between a stroke
      and an initial hook is shown by writing a
      small circle for the dot vowel, either after
      or before the stroke.
   (*b*) An intervening dash vowel, or a diphthong,
      is shown by intersecting the sign for the
      vowel or diphthong.

CHAPTER XIII

CIRCLE OR LOOP PRECEDING INITIAL HOOK

S before Straight Strokes Hooked for R. 76. Initial *s*, or *sw*, or *st*, preceding a straight stroke hooked for *r*, is expressed by writing the circle or loop on the same side as the *r* hook, that is, with the Right motion; thus, ⟋ *pry*, ⟋ *spry*; ⌐ *tray*, ⌐ *stray*; ⟋ *crew*, ⟋ *screw*; ⌐ *eater*, ⟍ *sweeter*; ⌐ *utter*, ⌐ *stutter*; ⌐ *ochre*, ⌐ *stoker*.

S before other Hooked Strokes. 77. In other cases *s* is written inside the initial hook, so that both circle and hook are clearly shown; thus, ⟍ *offer*, ⟍ *suffer*, ⟍ *sever*, ⟍ *deceiver*, ⟍ *soother*, ⟍ *sinner*, ⟍ *prisoner*, ⟍ *plies*, ⟍ *supplies*, ⟍ *possible*, ⟍ *pedestal*, ⟍ *settle*, ⟍ *satchel*, ⟍ *sickle*, ⟍ *bicycle*, ⟍ *exclaim*, ⟍ *evil*, ⟍ *civil*, ⟍ *prosper*, ⟍ *offspring*, ⟍ *destroy*, ⟍ *extra*, ⟍ *mystery*, ⟍ *nostrum*, ⟍ *lisper*, ⟍ *reciter*, ⟍ *wiseacre*.

(*a*) Where *l* hook cannot be clearly shown in the middle of a word, the stroke *l* is written; thus, ⟍ *forcible*, ⟍ *unsaddle*, ⟍ *musical*.

(*b*) When *skr* or *sgr* follows *t* or *d*, the circle is written with the Left motion; thus, ⌐ *tacker*, ⌐ *Tasker*; ⌐ *degree*, ⌐ *disagree*; ⌐ *digress*,

58

⌐ *disgrace.* When *skr* occurs after *p* or *b*, the hook *r* may be omitted; thus, ⟍ᵥ *prescribe,* ⟍ᵥ *subscriber.*

Exercise 47

Read, copy, and transcribe

1. [shorthand outlines]

2. [shorthand outlines]

3. [shorthand outlines]

4. [shorthand outlines]

5. [shorthand outlines]

Exercise 48

Write in Shorthand

1. Set, setter, settle, stab, stabber, sable, sweet, sweeter, sweetly, seek, seeker, sickle.
2. Supreme, sublime, cider, sidle, sacred, seclude.
3. Traceable, disclosure, plausible, classical, distressed, extremity, Tasker, task.
4. Suffers, simmers, sinners, peacefully, explosive, expels, risible, rasper.
5. Disgraces, discloses, prescribes, crossways.

GRAMMALOGUES

⟍ *from;*   ⟍ *very;*   ⟩ *there, their;*   ⌒ *more,*
remark-ed,   ⌒ *mere, Mr.;*   ‥‥ *nor,*   ⌣ *near;*
⟍ *surprise,*   ⟍ *surprised;*   ⌐ *sure;*   ⟩ *pleasure.*

PHRASE

⟩ *they are.*

Exercise 49

Read, copy, and transcribe

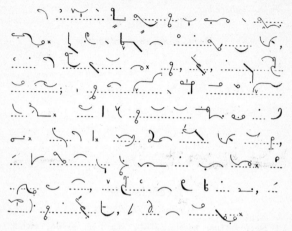

Exercise 50

Write in Shorthand

We-are surprised to know *from-your* favour *of-the* sixth *of* August *of-the* extremely long delay *in-the delivery of-the* Surrey *and* Gloucestershire books. So far *as-we-can* discover, *there-is-*no very clear reason *for-the* delay. *We-have* looked *into-the* case, *as you-*may-be-sure, *and it-is* still *a* mystery. *Mr.* Strong, *our* dispatch clerk, expressly disclaims *any* blame, *but,* if-possible, *he-will* take *more care with-the* books still *to-come.* He-will personally supervise *the* addressing *of-the* parcels. By-*the* way, *we* hope *to-have-the* new Uxbridge book ready *very* soon. *It-*will-*be in-the* same style *as our* classical library.

Summary

1. The circles *s* and *sw* and the loop *st* are prefixed to the straight strokes hooked for *r* by writing the circle or loop with the Right motion.

2. The circle *s* is prefixed to all other initially hooked strokes by writing the circle inside the hook, so that both the circle and hook are clearly shown.

3. The circle in words like *tusker* and *disgrace* is written with the Left motion ; but when *skr* follows *p* or *b*, the *r* is omitted.

CHAPTER XIV

N AND F HOOKS

N Hook. 78. A small final hook, struck by the Right motion ↺ adds *n* to all straight strokes; thus, ⌐⌐ *Ben*, ⌐ *tone*, ⌐ *chain*, ⌐ *coin*, ⌐ *rain*, ⌐ *hone*.

79. The hook which represents *r* at the beginning of a straight stroke, and that which represents *n* at the end, are both struck by the Right motion; thus, ⌐ *brain*, ⌐ *train*, ⌐ *crane*.

80. A small final hook, written inside the curve, adds *n* to all curved strokes; thus, ⌐ *fain*, ⌐ *thin*, ⌐ *assign*, ⌐ *shine*, ⌐ *moon*, ⌐ *lean*.

F-V Hook. 81. A small final hook, struck by the Le︠ft motion ↻, adds *f* or *v* to all straight strokes; thus, ⌐ *buff*, ⌐ *tough*, ⌐ *chafe*, ⌐ *cave*, ⌐ *rave*, ⌐ *hive*.

82. The hook which represents *l* at the beginning of a straight stroke, and that which represents *f* or *v* at the end, are both struck by the Le︠ft motion; thus, ⌐ *bluff*, ⌐ *cliff*, ⌐ *glove*.

83. There is no *f* or *v* hook to curves; therefore the stroke *f* or *v* must always be employed if *f* or *v* follows a curved stroke. The following pairs of words illustrate this: ⌐ *fine*, ⌐ *five*; ⌐ *line*, ⌐ *live*; ⌐ *nine*, ⌐ *knife*; ⌐ *moon*, ⌐ *move*.

84. A final hook cannot be employed when the word ends with a vowel sound, because a final vowel

requires a final stroke (par. 47). Compare ⟍ *pen* and ⟍ *penny;* ⟍ *puff* and ⟍ *puffy;* ⟍ *fun* and ⟍ *funny;* ⌒ *men* and ⌒ *many.*

LN and SH N. 85. The hooked forms *ln* and *sh n* when joined to another stroke may be written upward or downward; thus, ⟋ *gallon,* ⟋ *melon;* ⟋ *fallen,* ⟋ *aniline;* ⟋ *situation,* ⟋ *extenuation.*

Hooks used Medially. 86. The *n* and *f* hooks may be employed medially when they join easily and clearly with the following stroke; thus, ⟩ *plenty,* ⟋ *agent,* ⟋ *suddenness,* ⟩ *punish,* ⟩ *painful,* ⟋ *defence,* ⟋ *divide,* ⟋ *refer,* ⟋ *graphic.* If these outlines are compared with the following, it will be observed that a stroke is often used medially in preference to a hook in order to secure more facile outlines, or for purposes of distinction: ⟍ *brandy,* ⟋ *agency,* ⟋ *suddenly,* ⟍ *pronounce,* ⟍ *painless,* ⟋ *reviewer,* ⟋ *gravity.*

Syllable -NER. 87. The hook *n* and downward *r* are used for the representation of the final syllable *-ner* when following a straight upstroke; in all other cases, the syllable is represented by the sign ⌣ ; thus, ⟍ *opener,* ⟋ *joiner,* ⌣ *keener,* ⟋ *liner;* but ⟋ *runner,* ⟋ *winner,* ⟍ *yawner.*

N and F Hooks in Phraseography. 88. The *n* hook is sometimes used in phraseography for the words *been, than, on,* and *own,* and the *f-v* hook for the words *have* and *of;* thus, ⟍ *I have been,* ⟍ *I had been,* ⟍ *better than,* ⟋ *carried on,* ⟩ *their own,* ⟋ *our own,* ⟋ *which have,* ⊣ *out of.*

Exercise 51

Read, copy, and transcribe

1.
2.
3.
4.
5.

Exercise 52

Write in Shorthand

1. Open, opening, tune, tuning, dine, dining, strain.
2. Begin, beginning, run, runner, win, winner, join.
3. Fan, fancy, fin, finish, vain, vanish, mean, meanness, noun, renown.
4. Pave, paving, prove, provide, provoke, chaff, chaffinch, refer, referring, preserve.
5. Pen, penny, deaf, defy, fun, funny, men, many.

GRAMMALOGUES

⟍ *been ;* ⟋ *general-ly ;* ⟨ *within ;* ⟨ *southern ;* ⟍ *northern ;* ⟍ *behalf ;* ⎩ *advantage,* ⊣ *difficult.*

Exercise 53

Read, copy, and transcribe

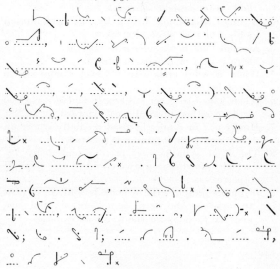

Exercise 54

Write in Shorthand

Local authorities, *as* borough *and* urban councils, *generally* derive *their* main revenue *from-the* rates they levy. They-may, *of*-course, receive profits *from any* business carried-*on* by-*them within-the* borough. *Over and* above *all-this* they receive allowances *from-the* state. Either men or women may appeal *to-the* authorities, *and*-they *very* often *do*, if-they *think* they-*have-been* unfairly assessed. *But it-will-be difficult for-them to* obtain relief unless they-*are* able *to*-prove *their* case, *and* satisfy-*the* authorities *as to a* supposed *overcharge*.

5—(*M*)

Summary

1. A small final hook struck by the Right motion adds *n* to straight strokes.

2. A small final hook struck by the LeFt motion adds *f* or *v* to straight strokes.

3. A small final hook adds *n* to curves.

4. There is no *f* or *v* hook to curves.

5. When a word ends with a vowel a final stroke must be used.

6. When joined to other strokes, *ln* and *sh n* may be written either upward or downward.

7. Hooks *n*, *f* or *v* may be used medially where an easy and legible joining is secured.

8. The final syllable *-ner* is represented by ⌣ when following any stroke except the straight upstrokes.

9. In phraseography, the *n* hook is sometimes used to represent the words *been*, *than*, *on*, and *own*, and the *f-v* hook for the words *have* and *of*.

CHAPTER XV

CIRCLES AND LOOPS TO FINAL HOOKS

Straight Strokes followed by NS, etc. 89. The sound of *s* or *ses*, *st* or *str* is added to the hook *n* attached to a straight stroke by writing the circle or loop on the same side as the hook, that is, with the Right motion, as ⌡ *Dan*, ⌡ *dance*, ⌡ *dances*, ⌡ *danced*, ⌡ *Dunster;* ＼ *pen*, ＼ *pens*, ＼ *expense*, ＼ *expenses;* ＼ *spin*, ＼ *spins*, ＼ *spinster*, ＼ *spinsters;* ⌐ *glen*, ⌐ *glens*, ⌐ *glances*, ⌐ *glanced;* ⌡ *dispense*, ⌡ *dispenses*, ⌡ *dispensed*.

Curves followed by NS, etc. 90. (*a*) The small circle (representing the sound of *z*) is added to the hook *n* attached to curves by writing the circle inside the hook; thus, ＼ *fine*, ＼ *fines;* ＼ *vines*, ＼ *frowns*, ⌐ *thrones*, ⌐ *shines*, ＼ *balloons*, ⌐ *earns*, ⌐ *zones*, ⌐ *mines*, ⌐ *nines*, ⌐ *lawns* The effect of the preceding rule is that the hook *n* and the small circle attached to a curve represent in all cases the *heavy* sound of *nz*, as in the words *fens* (nz), *vans* (nz), *Athens* (nz), *zones* (nz), *shines* (nz), *shrines* (nz), *moans* (nz), *nouns* (nz), *loans* (nz), *earns* (nz).

67

(b) Where the light sound of *ns* follows a curve, as in the word *fence*, it is expressed by ⌣; thus, ⌣ *fence*, ⌣ *evince*, ⌣ *lance*, ⌣ *mince*, ⌣ *thence*, ⌣ *nonce*. The effect of this rule is that the construction of outlines is regular in all related words of this class, so that the transcription of the forms is facilitated; thus, ⌣ *fence*, ⌣ *fences*, ⌣ *fenced*, ⌣ *fencing*; ⌣ *mince*, ⌣ *minces*, ⌣ *minced*, ⌣ *mincer*, ⌣ *mincing*; ⌣ *evince*, ⌣ *evinces*, ⌣ *evinced*, ⌣ *evincing*.

Circle S added to F-V Hooks.

91. The circle *s* is added to the hook *f* or *v* by writing the circle inside the hook; thus, ⌣ *puff*, ⌣ *puffs*, ⌣ *caves*, ⌣ *waves*, ⌣ *heaves*, ⌣ *operatives*, ⌣ *observes*, ⌣ *archives*, ⌣ *sheriffs*.

Medial NS or NZ.

92. When *ns* or *nz* occur medially both letters must be shown, as in the words ⌣ *pensive*, ⌣ *density*, ⌣ *chancel*, ⌣ *Johnson*, ⌣ *cancer*, ⌣ *cleanser*, ⌣ *fencer*, ⌣ *immensity*, ⌣ *rancid*, ⌣ *ransack*, ⌣ *wincer*, ⌣ *lonesome*, ⌣ *ransom*, ⌣ *winsome*, ⌣ *hansom*.

Exercise 55

Read, copy, and transcribe

1.
2.
3.
4.
5.
6.

Exercise 56

Write in Shorthand

1. Pence, expense, sixpence, sixpences, dispense, dispenses, dispensed.
2. Button, buttons, train, trains, entrance, entrances, entranced, disappearance, disappearances.
3. Shun, shuns, ocean, oceans, mean, means, linen, linens, saloon, saloons.
4. Reprieve, reprieves, native, natives, chief, chiefs, observe, observes.
5. Fence, offence, offences, immense, immensity, allowance, allowances, prominence.

GRAMMALOGUES

balance ;   circumstance ;   deliverance :
signify-ied-icant ;   significance ;   opinion.

Exercise 57

Read, copy, and transcribe

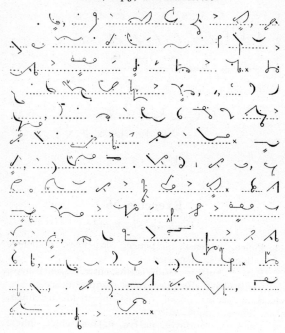

Exercise 58

Write in Shorthand

If I annoy *you in-the deliverance of-*my *opinion,
as-the* chances *are* I-may, *put it* down *to a* reading
man's reverence *for* books, *and-his* diligence *in-the*
pursuit *of a* course *which* lightens many *an hour
for-him. Think of-*these *significant* facts, *and your*
frowns may vanish. If-*you have a* love of books,

you-will feel no loneliness if *and when* men forget *you*.   *You-can* dispense *with-them in-the circumstances*;   *for-you*-will-*have within your*self, through-*the* brains *of-your* authors, many better men *to*-replace *them*.   *The balance of advantage in-the* change *is* likely *to be in-your* favour.   *You*-will grasp-*the significance of-this remark*, I-am-*sure*; *for-the* man *who* derives *pleasure from* reading books makes *for-himself* reserves *of* strength *to-call*-upon against *the* time *of*-trouble or stress.

Summary

1. The sound of *s* or *ses*, *st* or *str* is added to hook *n* attached to straight strokes by writing the circle or loop on the same side as the hook.
2. Circle *s* is added to straight strokes hooked for *f* or *v*, and to curves hooked for *n*, by writing the circle inside the hook.
3. The light sound of *ns* after a curve is expressed by the sign ‿ᵒ *ns*.
4. The heavy sound of *nz* after a curve is expressed by the circle *s* written inside the hook *n*.
5. When *ns* or *nz* occur medially both letters must be shown.

CHAPTER XVI

THE *SHUN* HOOK

The Termination -SHUN. 93. The termination *shun* or *zhun*, variously spelt -*tion*, -*sion*, -*cian*, -*tian*, -*sian*, etc., is represented by a large hook, to which circle *s* may be added as required, as, ⌒ *notion*, ⌒ *notions*, ⌐ *caution*, ⌐ *cautions*.

94. The *shun* hook is written inside curves ; thus, ⌐ *fashion*, ⌐ *fashions*, ⌐ *motion*, ⌐ *nation*, ⌐ *nations*.

95. (*a*) When added to a straight stroke with an initial attachment (circle, loop, or hook) the hook is written on the side *opposite* to the initial attachment, in order to preserve the straightness of the stroke ; thus, ⌐ *citation*, ⌐ *sections*, ⌐ *oppression*, ⌐ *Grecian*.

(*b*) The *shun* hook is written with the Right motion after the form ⌐ , light or heavy, and with the Left motion after the forms ⌐ ⌐ , in order that the *k* or *g* may be kept straight ; thus, ⌐ *affection*, ⌐ *vacation*, ⌐ *selection*, ⌐ *selections ;* and

96. On the side opposite to the last vowel when following a straight stroke *without* an initial attachment, in order to indicate where the last vowel occurs ; thus, ⌐ *passion*, ⌐ *option*, ⌐ *action*, ⌐ *cautions*, ⌐ *occasion ;* but

72

(a) On the right side of | *t*, | *d*, / *j*, because it is known that the last vowel always occurs after these letters, and there is no need to indicate the fact, and also because the writing of the hook on the right-hand side of these letters carries the hand forward in readiness for the next word ; thus, ⌐ *rotation*, ⌐ *notation*, ⌐ *gradation*, ⌐ *logicians*.

Exercise 59

Read, copy, and transcribe

1.

2.

3.

4.

5.

6.

Exercise 60

Write in Shorthand

1. Erasion, invasions, division, elevation, mansion.
2. Solution, desolation, relations, stipulations.
3. Exception, impression, celebration, recitation, discussion, exclusion.
4. Specification, infection, navigation, relegation.
5. Occupation, Russian, occasion, education, obligation, lubrication.
6. Deputation, adaptation, imitation, presentation.

Shun following Circles S and NS. 97. When *shun* follows the circle *s* or circle *ns*, it is expressed by a small hook written on the opposite side to the circle and with the same motion ; thus, ⎸ *decision,* ⌡ *dispensation.*

(*a*) A third-place vowel between the circle and the *shun* hook is expressed by the vowel-sign being written outside the hook ; thus, ⟍ *position,* ⟍ *physician,* ⌐ *transition.* The circle *s* may be added thus, ⟍ *positions,* ⌐ *transitions.*

(*b*) When a second-place vowel is to be read between the circle and *shun* it need not be indicated ; thus, ⟍ *possession,* ⌐ *accession,* ⌐ *sensation.* First-place vowels do not occur between the circle and *shun.*

Shun Hook Medially. 98. The *shun* hook may be used medially ; thus, ⎰ *additional,* ⟍ *actionable,* ⎰ *devotional,* ⟍ *positional,* ⎰ *transitional.*

Words ending in -uation and -uition. 99. When a diphthong and a vowel occur immediately before *shun,* the stroke *sh* and the hook *n* must be written thus, ⎯⌐ *extenuation,* but ⎯⌐ *extension ;* ⌐ *intuition,* but ⎰ *notation.* This does not apply to such words as ⎯⌐ *accentuation,* ⟍⎰ *perpetuation,* where, in order to avoid a lengthy outline, the large hook is used.

Exercise 61

Read, copy, and transcribe

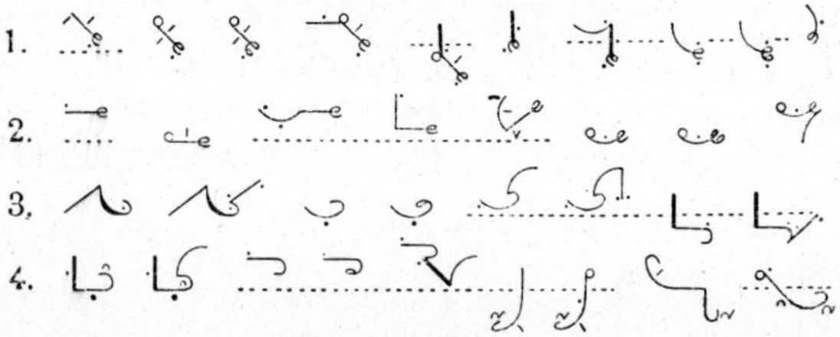

Exercise 62

Write in Shorthand

1. Proposition, propositions, precision, procession, processions.
2. Disposition, indisposition, accusation, accusations, vexation.
3. Mission, missions, missionary, commission, commissions, commissionaire, exception, exceptional.
4. Discretion, discretionary, affection, affectionate.

GRAMMALOGUES

subjective, *subjection*; *signification*; *information*; *satisfaction*, *justification*, *generalization*.

Exercise 63

Read, copy, and transcribe

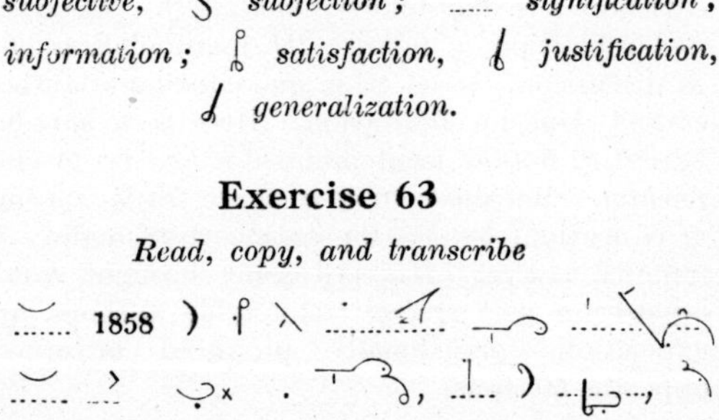

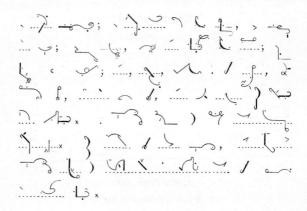

Exercise 64

Write in Shorthand

Lord Macaulay *was* blessed *with-the* possession *of* rare powers *of*-memory. *His* accumulation *of* facts *was* immense. He-*was* almost *in a* state *of subjection to-his* memory, *and a subjective* examination *of-the information in-his* possession at *any*-time *would have-been* a revelation even *to-himself.* *The* retention *and* repetition *of* figures, *the* manipulation *of* facts *in* discussion, *the* selection *and* citation *of* authorities caused *him* no hesitation. He-*was to-have-been a* barrister, *but-the* legal profession *had* no fascination *for-him.* Macaulay took *a* share *in-the* promotion *of* education, *but-his* reputation rests mainly *on-his* famous essays. *His* criticisms brought *him into* opposition *with several* fashionable authors, *and-his* expositions occasionally produced bitterness *in* opposite factions.

Summary

The hook -*shun* is written—

To curves	Inside the curve.
To straight strokes with initial attachment	On the side opposite to the initial attachment.
To *k* and *g* following the curves ⟍ ⟍ ⟋ (up)	With the Left or Right motion as required to keep the *k* or *g* straight.
To straight strokes other than *t*, *d* or *j* without initial attachment	On the side opposite to the last vowel.
To *t*, *d* and *j* without initial attachment	On the right side.
Following the circles *s* or *ns*	On the side opposite to the circle.
Finally	In *punctuation* and a few similarly long words.
Medially	Like the other hooks.

CHAPTER XVII

THE ASPIRATE

Upward H. 100. The upward form of *h* is employed in the great majority of cases, because it joins more readily with other strokes and abbreviations ; as, ⟋ *hope*, ⟋ *head*, ⟋ *hatch*, ⟋ *hedge*, ⟋ *hush*, ⟋ *honey*, ⟋ *hung*, ⟋ *hero*, ⟋ *hearth*, ⟋ *hose*, ⟋ *husk*, ⟋ *hisses*, ⟋ *haste*, ⟋ *hove*, ⟋ *hen*, ⟋ *Henry*, ⟋ *hackle*, ⟋ *hawker*, ⟋ *hammer*, ⟋ *upheave*, ⟋ *behead*, ⟋ *adhesive*, ⟋ *Jehovah*, ⟋ *overhaul*, ⟋ *enhance*, ⟋ *rehearse*.

Downward H. 101. The downward form of *h* is used

(*a*) When *h* stands alone, as in ⟋ *hay*, ⟋ *high*, and in compounds and derivatives like ⟋ *haystack*, ⟋ *higher*, ⟋ *highly* ;

(*b*) When *h* is followed by ⎯ *k* or ⎯ *g* ; as, ⟋ *hawk*, ⟋ *hog* ;

(*c*) When *h* follows upward *l* or a horizontal stroke ; as, ⟋ *Lahore*, ⟋ *coherence*, ⟋ *mahogany*, ⟋ *unhook*.

Following S, etc. 102. (*a*) In a few words like ⟋ *Soho* and ⟋ *Sheehy*, the circle of *h* is written inside the curve ; and in such words as ⟋ *Fitzhugh*, and ⟋ *racehorse*, where *s* and *h* occur medially, the circle is enlarged for the representation of *s*.

78

(*b*) When *h* follows another stroke, it must be written so that it cannot be misread for *s ch* or *sr*; thus, ⸻ *cohere*, but ⸻ *exchequer*; ⸻ *abhor*, but ⸻ *observer*.

Tick H. 103. (*a*) When preceding strokes ⸻ *m*, ⸻ *l*, ⸻ *r*, initial *h* is represented by a short tick, written in the direction of downward *h*; thus, ⸻ *home*, ⸻ *healthy*, ⸻ *harm*.

(*b*) The tick *h* may be employed medially in phrasing, but not in words; thus, ⸻ *for whom*, ⸻ *of her*, ⸻ *to her*; but ⸻ *inhuman*, ⸻ *overhaul*.

Dot H. 104. Where a stroke form of *h* is not convenient in the middle of a word, *h* is represented by placing a light dot before the vowel which is to be aspirated; thus, ⸻ *apprehensive*, ⸻ *perhaps*, ⸻ *vehicle*, ⸻ *hogshead*, ⸻ *uphill*, ⸻ *downhill*, ⸻ *manhood*.

Exercise 65

Read, copy, and transcribe

Exercise 66

Write in Shorthand

1. Head, hitch, huge, hyphen, hurry, hurries.
2. Host, hone, heave, hovel, haggle, hence, hover, boyhood, prohibition, cohesive.
3. Hack, hackney, hawk, Hawkins, hoax, cohere, high, higher.
4. Home, hall, hallow, hire, neighbourhood, freehold.

Phrases

Dear Sir, *yours truly,* *every circumstance,* *all circumstances,* *you will remember,* *I believe,* *I will tell you,* *I am surprised.*

Exercise 67

Read, copy, and transcribe

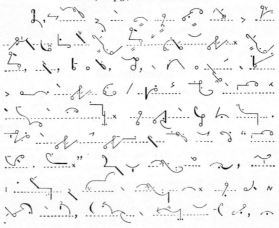

Exercise 68

Write in Shorthand

Dear-Sir,—*The* heavy mahogany table *for-your* new home, "Hillside," Woodhouse Lane, *is* ready *for delivery* at *any*-time *when-we* hear *from-you*. *We* hope *to-have-the* hangings fixed *to*-morrow, *and-the* curtains hung by Wednesday *next*. *The* new hammocks *and* hassocks *are almost* ready, *and*-they-will-be *delivered next* week. *Our* van may-*be in-your* neighbourhood *on*-Monday, *in-which*-case *you shall-have-the* hall *chairs and-the* whole *of-the* small household *things* then. *But for a* mishap at *our* Harley Works, *you would-have had-the* hair cushions *for-the* settee before *this*. *We* hope, *however*, *to*-receive *them on*-Friday, *and to-deliver them with-the* other *things on*-Monday. *Yours*-truly,

Summary

1. The upward form of *h* is most commonly used.
2. The downward form is written when *h* is the only stroke in the word and in compounds and derivatives like *hayrick*, *high-flown*; also before *k* or *g*.
3. The tick *h* is written initially to ⌒ ⌢ ⌍ The word HoMeLieR forms a useful mnemonic.
4. The dot *h* is used as an alternative to the stroke in the middle of a word.

CHAPTER XVIII

UPWARD AND DOWNWARD *R*

In order to present a complete statement of the rules for the writing of the alternative forms of *r*, the directions given to the student in par. 27 are repeated here.

Vowel preceding R. 105. When initial *r* is preceded by a vowel, the downward form is used; thus, ⟍ *air*, ⟍ *airy*, ⟍ *erase*, ⟍ *ire*, ⟍ *Irish*, ⟍ *orb*.

Vowel following R. 106. In other cases, the general rule is to write initial or final *r* upward when it is followed by a vowel, and downward when it is not followed by a vowel; thus, ⟍ *rob*, ⟍ *borrow*; ⟍ *rainy*, ⟍ *narrow*; ⟍ *carry*, ⟍ *car*; ⟍ *furrow*, ⟍ *fur*; ⟍ *sorry*, ⟍ *soar*; ⟍ *story*, ⟍ *store*; ⟍ *ware*, ⟍ *wary*; ⟍ *siren*, ⟍ *stern*.

107. Initial *r* followed by *m* is always written downward, because of the easier outline thus obtained; as, ⟍ *roam*, ⟍ *ram*.

108. Facility of outline is of the utmost importance, however, and accordingly either form of *r* is written, and vowel indication ignored, in order to secure a facile form. The upper form is written, therefore, in ⟍ *irate*, ⟍ *arch*, ⟍ *urge*, ⟍ *earth*, ⟍ *oracle*, and similar words where *r* is immediately followed by | *t*, | *d*, / *ch*, / *j*, (*th* or ⟍ *k*, ⟍ *gl*, ⟍ *w*.

109. Generally, the upward form is preferable after two downstrokes; as, ⟍ *prepare*, ⟍ *trampler*,

82

Shakespeare, because the hand is thereby carried back to the line of writing. But the downward form is better in ⟍⟍⟍⟍ *pinafore*, ⟋ *shuffler*, ⟋ *persevere*, etc., because of the easier joining with the preceding *f* or *v*.

110. After a single straight upstroke, the upward form is easier, because it avoids an angle ; thus, ⟋ *roar*, ⟋ *aware*, ⟋ *yore* ; but the suffix -*er* must be written with downward *r* in ⟋ *roarer*, ⟋ *rarer*, because a treble-length straight upstroke would not be easily readable.

111. The upward form is obviously better in ⟋ *officer*, ⟋ *nicer*, ⟋ *closer*, ⟋ *razor*, where *r* immediately follows a curve and circle like ⟍ or ⟍ , or a straight horizontal or upstroke circled for *s*.

R Finally Hooked. 112. When *r* follows another stroke and is hooked finally, it is generally written upward ; thus, ⟍ *spurn*, ⟍ *fern*, ⟍ *portion*.

Medial R. 113. Medial *r* is generally written upward ; as in ⟍ *park*, ⟍ *parsnip*, ⟍ *terrify*, ⟍ *mark*, ⟍ *roared* ; but the downward form is retained in some derivative words, as, ⟍ *powerful*, ⟍ *barely*, ⟍ *disarrange* ; and the use of the alternative forms provides a distinction in pairs of words such as ⟍ *clerk*, ⟍ *cleric*.

Exercise 69

Read, copy, and transcribe

1.
2.
3.
4.
5.

6.

7.

Exercise 70

Write in Shorthand

1. Ear, era, erase, argue, oral, Eric, early.
2. Retire, retrace, review, reviewing, rose, roses, rank.
3. Paris, diary, gallery, victory, assurance, memory.
4. Answer, censor, cruiser, origin, turn, Lucerne.
5. Perth, veracity, parade, terrible, forty, firm.

PHRASES AND CONTRACTIONS

by all, by all means; at all, at all costs; in our, in our opinion; everything, something; anything, nothing.

Exercise 71

Read, copy, and transcribe

Exercise 72

Write in Shorthand

The food eaten by man bears *something* like-*the* same relation *to-his* power *of* working *as-the* coal thrown *into-the* furnace bears *to-the* engine *which* drives *the* rotary press, or draws *the* train. *The* power *in-our* arms or *in-our* brains *is* rightly said *to be* produced *in-our* stomach, *and it-is from-the* same organ *we* derive *the* force necessary *to*-rouse us *to* severe exertion *in-the* earning *of-the* wage or salary *we* receive *for our* services. *Something of-the* value *of-our* work rests upon-*the* strength producing value *of-our* food. At-*all*-costs, *and* by-*all*-means, *we should* take measures *to* ensure-*the* food value *of* *everything we* eat.

Summary

Initial *r*	Written downward when preceded by a vowel, and initially before *m* ; as ⟍ *erase*, ⟍ *room*.
Initial or Final *r*	Written upward when followed by a vowel, and downward when not followed by a vowel, as ⟋ *race*, ⟍ *parry*, ⟍ *air*, ⟍ *par*.
Medial *r*	Generally written upward ; but downward in some derivatives.
When hooked and following another stroke	Generally written upward ; as, ⟍ *burn*, ⟍ *mourn*.
For an easier outline	Written either upward or downward irrespective of vowels ; as, ⟋ *earth*, ⟍ *answer*, ⟍ *deplore*, ⟍ *debar*.

CHAPTER XIX

UPWARD AND DOWNWARD *L* AND *SH*

Upward L. 114. The stroke *l*, whether initial or final, is most commonly written upward ; as in ⌢ *lapse*, ⌄ *spell*, ⌐ *load*, ⌐ *delay*, ⌐ *allege*, ⌐ *jelly*, ⌐ *lake*, ⌐ *coal*, ⌐ *loaf*, ⌐ *fellow*, ⌐ *loathe*, ⌐ *Othello*, ⌐ *Lacey*, ⌐ *assail*, ⌐ *sale*, ⌐ *stale*, ⌐ *leisure*, ⌐ *shallow*.

L preceding or following Curve and Circle. 115. When *l* immediately precedes or follows a circle which is attached to a curve, it is written in the same direction as the circle ; thus, ⌐ *lesson*, ⌐ *nasal*, ⌐ *elusive*, ⌐ *vessel*, ⌐ *losing*, ⌐ *Kingsley*, ⌐ *lissom*.

L after N and NG. 116. After the strokes ⌐ *n* and ⌐ *ng*, final *l* is written downward so as to avoid a change of motion ; as in ⌐ *only*, ⌐ *wrongly*, ⌐ *manly* ; and the downward form is retained in derivatives ; as, ⌐ *manliness*, ⌐ *enlisting*.

L and Vowel Indication. 117. For the purpose of vowel indication, initial *l* is written downward when preceded by a vowel and followed immediately by a horizontal, not hooked or circled initially ; thus, ⌐ *alike* but ⌐ *like* ; ⌐ *alone* but ⌐ *loan* ; ⌐ *along* but ⌐ *long* : ⌐ *elm* but ⌐ *lame*.

118. Also for the purpose of vowel indication, final *l* is written upward after ⌣ *f*, ⌣ *v*, ⌒ *sk*, or a straight upstroke when a vowel follows *l*, and downward when no vowel follows *l* ; thus, ⌣ *follow* but ⌣ *fall ;* ⌣ *valley* but ⌣ *vale ;* ⌒ *scaly* but ⌒ *scale ;* ⌣ *ruly* but ⌒ *rule.*

Medial L. 119. Medial *l* is generally written upward ; but either form is used for an easier joining ; thus, ⌣ *unload* but ⌣ *unlock ;* ⌣ *vulgar* but ⌣ *overlook ;* ⌣ *facility* but ⌣ *film.*

Upward and Downward Sh. 120. (*a*) The curve ⌐ *sh*, joined to another curve, generally follows the motion of that curve ; thus, ⌣ *fish*, ⌐ *smash*, ⌐ *lash ;* but it is written *downward* after the curve ⌣ *n ;* thus, ⌐ *gnash.* When joined to a straight stroke, *sh* is generally written downward ; thus, ⌐ *push*, ⌐ *cherish*, ⌐ *shake*, ⌐ *sherry ;* but it is written *upward* after the heavy stroke │ *d*, as in ⌐ *dash.*

(*b*) After a straight down stroke with an initial attachment, *sh* is generally written on the opposite side to such attachment ; thus, ⌐ *spacious*, ⌐ *blush*, ⌐ *brush.* In other cases the form is used which gives the easier joining ; as in ⌐ *sugar*, ⌐ *shackle*, ⌐ *chauffeur*, ⌐ *shovel.*

Exercise 73

Read, copy, and transcribe

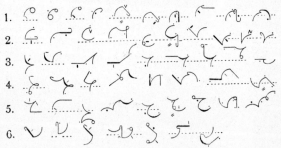

Exercise 74

Write in Shorthand

1. Lie, lies, sly, slice, slices, steel, stolen, swallow.
2. Alps, Alaska, loth, loafer, lore, locker, latch.
3. Alack, lack, allocation, location, license, Allison.
4. Bale, billow, towel, Filey, veal, villa, dwell.
5. Canals, denial, frowningly, vessel, profusely.
6. Unlucky, lucky, pulling, spelling, sculling.
7. Plush, splash, crush, atrocious, waspish.

PHRASES

as is ; is as ; this is ; last year ; at first ; just now.

Exercise 75

Read, copy, and transcribe

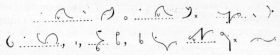

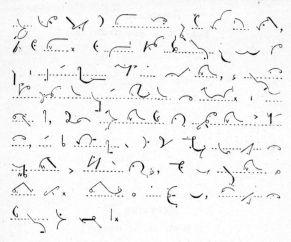

Exercise 76

Write in Shorthand

Dear-Sir,

　The volumes *of-the* French Revolution *for-which-you* ask *in-your* favour *of-the* first July *shall-be delivered to-you* early *to*-morrow. *We-are* just-now out-*of* stock *of-the* " Life *of* Lord Lumley," last-*year's* best seller, *and we-are* unable *to* say *when-we-shall* receive copies. *We-have a* daily *delivery from-the* wholesalers, *however, and you*-may-rely upon *our* mailing-*the* volume *to-you as*-soon-*as it* reaches us. *We-are* taking-*the liberty of* enclosing *for-your* approval " Naval Lessons *of-the* War," by Philip Bailey. Please return *this with-the next* parcel if -*it* makes no appeal *to-you. Yours*-truly,

Summary

1. The upward form of *l* is most commonly written.
2. When immediately preceding or following a circle which is attached to a curve, *l* follows the direction of the circle.
3. Final *l* is written downward after *n* and *ng*, and derivatives of words similar to *manly*.
4. When preceded by a vowel and followed immediately by a horizontal, initial *l* is written downward.
5. After ⌣ *f*, ⌣ *v*, ⌒ *sk*, or a straight upstroke, final *l* is written upward when followed by a vowel, and downward when not followed by a vowel.
6. Medial *l* is generally written upward.
7. Stroke *sh*, following a straight downstroke having an initial attachment, is written opposite to the initial attachment. In other cases the form is used which gives the better joining.

CHAPTER XX

COMPOUND CONSONANTS

Initial W. 121. A *large* initial hook adds *w* to *k* — and — *g*; thus, ⌐ *keen,* ⌐ *queen,* ⌐ *Gwynn.*

Initial WH. 122. A *small* initial hook to *l* represents *w*, and a *large* initial hook to *l* represents *wh*; thus, (*ell,* (*well,* (*whale.*

Strokes L and R Thickened. 123. Downward *l* is thickened for the addition of *r* preceded by any lightly sounded vowel, and downward *r* is thickened for the addition of *-er* only; thus, ⟩ *vale,* ⟩ *valour;* ↘ *hire,* ↘ *hirer.*

Addition of P or B to M. 124. The curve ⌒ *m* is thickened for the addition of *p* or *b*; thus, ⌒ *hem,* ⌒ *hemp,* ⌒ *moss,* ⌒ *emboss.*

Aspirated W. 125. The aspirate is added to ⌣ *w* by enlarging the hook; thus, ⌣ *weasel,* ⌣ *whistle,* ⌣ *aware,* ⌣ *where.*

Stroke L after KW. 126. After ⌐ *kw, l* is written upward when followed by a vowel, and downward when not followed by a vowel; thus, ⌐ *squally,* ⌐ *squall.*

Vowel preceding W. 127. The initial hooks in *wl* and *whl* are read *first*. Therefore, if a vowel precedes *w*, the stroke form of *w* or *wh* must be written, and not the hook; thus, ⌐ *while,* ⌐ *awhile.*

Use of LR and RR Signs. 128. The form of *l* or *r* which is used in the root word is retained in the derivative ; thus, ⌇ *boil*, ⌇ *boiler*, ⌇ *mill*, ⌇ *miller ;* ⌇ *full*, ⌇ *fuller ;* ⌇ *snare*, ⌇ *snarer.* The use of ⌇ *rer* is strictly confined to derivatives of words written with downward *r*.

Vowel after Final R. 129. The thickened forms ⌇ *lr*, ⌇ *rr* must not be written finally if a vowel follows *r ;* compare ⌇ *fuller* with ⌇ *foolery ;* ⌇ *valour* with ⌇ *valorous.*

Hooked Form of MP. 130. An initial or final hook may be attached to the sign ⌒ ; as in ⌇ *scamper*, ⌇ *hempen*, ⌇ *ambition.* The sign ⌒ is not used when *pr*, *br*, *pl* or *bl* immediately follows *m.* Compare ⌇ *empress* with ⌇ *emperor ;* ⌇ *embrace* with ⌇ *embower ;* ⌇ *imply* with ⌇ *impel ;* ⌇ *emblem* with ⌇ *embolden.*

Exercise 77

Read, copy, and transcribe

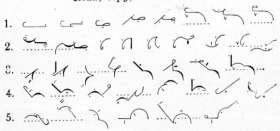

Exercise 78

Write in Shorthand

1. Quake, earthquake, square, liquid, liquidation, require, Maguire.
2. Wall, wallflower, welfare, will, willing, unwilling, while, awhile, jump, romp.
3. Fairer, scorer, scaler, nowhere, whisper, whimper.
4. Imprison, umbrella, taller, similar, failure.

GRAMMALOGUES

✓ *whether* ; ⌐ *impossible* ; ⌐ *important-ance*, ⌒ *improve-d-ment*.

Exercise 79

Read, copy, and transcribe

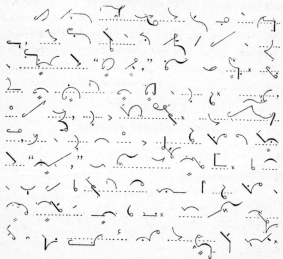

Exercise 80

Write in Shorthand

I-*have*-no *wish* *to* impose my views upon-*the*
ambassador, or *to* embarrass *him* by asking *for*
impossible improvements ; but it-is important I *should*
impress upon *him the* chancellor's *opinion in-the*
case *of-those* lumber vessels. *You*-will-see *how*
imperative *it-is* I *should* see-*the* ambassador, if-
we-are to-have any improvement *in-our* relations just-
now. I-desire *to* discover *whether-the* whaler's
story *is* true, or-*the* idle tale *of a* wilful imposter.
I-*shall* occupy only *a* quarter *of an hour, and*-I-am-
sure *the* ambassador will agree *the importance of-the*
case *is* well worth-*the* time.

Summary

1. Table of compound consonants—

Character	Name	Letters	As in
⌐	kwā	QU	**qu**ick, re**qu**est
⌐	gwā	GU	**gu**ava, lin**gu**al
⌐ (up)	wel	WL	**w**ail, un**well**
⌐ (up)	hwel	WHL	**wh**ale, mean**while**
⌐ (down)	ler	LR	fee**ler**, scho**larly**
⌐ (down)	rer	RR	poo**rer**, sha**rer**
⌐	{emp} {emb}	MP, MB	ca**mp**, **emb**alm
⌐	hwa	WH	**wh**ere, every**wh**ere

2. After ⊂ *kw* stroke *l* is written upward when followed by a vowel, and downward when not followed by a vowel.

3. The initial hooks to *l* are always read first.

4. When the downward forms of *l* or *r* are written in root words, the thickened forms ⌒ *lr,* ⌐ *rr* are written in the derived words.

5. The thickened forms ⌒ *lr,* ⌐ *rr* must not be used when a vowel follows *r*.

6. The sign ⌢ is not used when *m* is immediately followed by *pr, br, pl* or *bl*.

CHAPTER XXI

VOWEL INDICATION

Vowels Implied. 131. A careful reading of the rules governing the use of the circles, loops, and hooks will have led the student to realize (a) that when a word begins or ends with a consonant, that consonant is to be written with the briefest form; as, ⵡ soup, ⵡ place, ⵡ spinsters, ⵡ dances, ⵡ craves, unless there is a rule to the contrary, as in the words ⵡ Siam and ⵡ joyous; and (b) that when a word begins or ends with a vowel sound, the first or last consonant, as the case may be, must be represented by a stroke in order to accommodate the vowel-sign.

It will be seen from the foregoing that in very many words an initial or a final vowel may be *implied* by the outline of the word, without the use of the vowel-sign. The following illustrations will serve as additional examples of the implication of initial or final vowels.

INITIAL VOWEL IMPLIED

asleep,	assume,	arising,	arrives,	along.
alike,	aware,	awake,	awhile,	awoke.

INITIAL CONSONANT IMPLIED

sleep,	sum,	rising,	raves,	long.
like,	wear,	wake,	while,	woke.

FINAL VOWEL IMPLIED

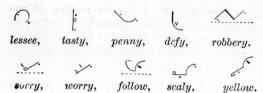

lessee,   tasty,   penny,   defy,   robbery.

sorry,   worry,   follow,   scaly,   yellow.

FINAL CONSONANT IMPLIED

less,   taste,   pen,   deaf,   repair.

sore,   wore,   fall,   scale,   yell.

In many of the words given in the following exercises an initial or a final vowel is suggested by the outline employed.

Exercise 81

Read, copy, and transcribe

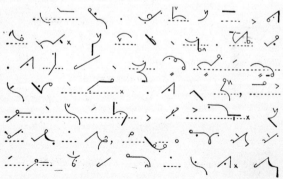

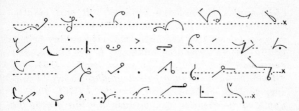

Exercise 82

Write in Shorthand

The judge *in-his* charge *to-the* jury said : *This* poor boy's injury *is very* severe, *and-if what-he* states *is* right, *it-was* due *to-the* absence *of a* hooter *on-the* car *which* Robinson drove along-*the* arcade at *a very* fast rate, *his* speed, *if-we-can* take-*the* story *of-the* police *as* correct, *being* at-least forty miles *an hour*, far *too* fast *in* so busy *a* thoroughfare. *The* boy says *the* car came *on* with *a* rush, no alarm *was given*, he-*was* struck *and*-thrown *with a* force so terrific *as to*-break *his* right leg. If-*you think his* story *is* right, *you*-will *give him* damages. If-*you* assume *his* story *is* wrong, *and*-if *it* appears *to-you the* injury *was* caused by *his own* lack *of* vigilance, *you*-will refuse *him the* damages *for-which* he asks. *You*-must *carefully* weigh both-*the* boy's case *and-the* case *as* set out by Robinson *and* decide *on-the* facts *as*-they appear *to-you.*

Revisionary Exercise (B)

Dear Dr. Fry,

By-*all*-means, apply *to-my people to-tell-you* of-*my* travels *during-the* past three *years.* I-*believe it*-will-*be* difficult *for-you to-believe all*-they-will-*tell-you*, *because-it-is* almost *beyond belief.* They-will-*tell-you a very* attractive story, *all-the more* striking *because of-its truth.* If-*you*-leave *your call till next* month, *there*-may-*be more to-tell-you, and-the* news items may-*be equal to anything you have* read. Every-day brings before-*me circumstances* unknown *to-me* before, *and* every *circumstance is* singular *in itself. It-is very difficult for-me to be surprised* at *anything* now. I-*am-surprised* at *nothing* at-*all*, nor do I-*think there-is anything to surprise me, because* my-life *during-the* past few *years has* brought *me* so-many *surprises from all* quarters. I-*have-been delivered from* troubles *when deliverance would* appear *to-have-been impossible, and when an improvement of-circumstances* looked *too difficult to be* possible. *You*-will-see-*the significance of-this when you* know *something of what* I-*have-been* through, *though-the* tale *can-be* no-*more* than *a mere generalization* or *general* review. Still, *it*-will-*be as near-the* facts *as* possible *in-the circumstances.* I-will-*tell-you and Mr.* Oliver *more when* I-see-*you, and it*-will-*be an advantage and an immense satisfaction to-me to-tell-you* both. *You*-will-then *be* at *liberty to* ask *for any number of* details, *and,* as-far-*as* I-am-able *to-remember them,* I-will *give them to-you.* I-*can* see *myself in-your* easy-*chair in-the larger of-your two* rooms at home, *with* my journal *on*-my knee *and-the cheer*ful listeners facing *me* while I-talk *of-the* days *of*-my *subjection and-of-the* dreary *subjective* examinations I gave *myself in justification of*-my actions. *In*-my *opinion, you*-will say-*the* tale *is significant, and, in signification of-the* happenings *in-the northern and southern* climes, far *beyond anything you* know. I-must leave-*the balance of-the* tale, *however, till* I-*can go over it with-you.* I-*have* some *information, largely* personal *to-you, which* I-must *tell-you* at-*all*-costs before long. I-trust *the information* will *give-you as-much-pleasure as* I-*think-it*-will. *Anyway it*-will enable *you to*-set *a* right *valuation* upon-*the* rest *of*-my story. Please *remember* me *to-the* children at home, *and to-the* older *and larger* children also. I-*shall-be* home again *within* six months. I-*shall* hope *to* see-*the principal members of-the* local literary club *within a* few days *of*-my return. Ever *yours*, Arthur Clyde.   (468 words)

Summary

1. An initial vowel requires the use of an initial stroke, in order to give a place for the vowel-sign : a final vowel requires the use of a final stroke, for the same reason.

2. An initial or a final vowel may frequently be indicated by the form written for the initial or final consonant.

3. Words beginning with the sound of a consonant have that consonant represented in the briefest form unless there is a rule to the contrary, as in the case of the word *Siam*.

4. Similarly, words ending with the sound of a consonant, or group of consonants, have the consonant or group represented in the briefest form.

CHAPTER XXII

THE HALVING PRINCIPLE (Section 1)

General Rule. 132. Halving a stroke in length indicates the addition of *t* or *d*. In words of one syllable, however, unless the stroke is finally hooked, or has a joined diphthong, a light stroke is halved for *t* only, and a heavy stroke for *d* only.

Halving for either T or D. 133. (*a*) In words of more than one syllable, a stroke may be halved for either *t* or *d;* thus, ⌒ *rabbit,* ⌒ *rapid;* ⌐ *credit,* ⌊ *debit;* ⋯⋯ *honoured,* ≅ *applied.*

(*b*) A stroke having a final hook or a joined diphthong may be halved for either *t* or *d ;* thus, ↘ *pave,* ↘ *paved;* ↓ *ten,* ↓ *tent* or *tend ;* ⌒ *men,* ⌒ *meant* or *mend ;* ⌐ *few,* ⌐ *feud ;* ↘ *prow,* ↘ *proud.*

Halving for T only, or for D only. 134. (*a*) In words of one syllable, light strokes, without a final hook or a joined diphthong, are halved for *t* only ; thus, ↘ *play,* ↘ *plate,* but ↘ *played;* ⌐ *thaw,* ⌐ *thought,* but ⌐ *thawed.*

(*b*) In words of one syllable, heavy strokes, without a final hook or a joined diphthong, are halved for *d* only ; thus, ↘ *bray,* ↘ *brayed,* but ↘ *bright ;* ⌐ *gray,* ⌐ *grade,* but ⌐ *greet.*

Vocalizing Half-length Forms. 135. (*a*) Vowel-signs to half-length forms are read next to the primary stroke : thus, ↘ *fie,* ↘ *fight ;* ↘ *off,* ↘ *oft ;* ⌐ *seek,* ⌐ *sect ;* ⌐ *seeker,* ⌐ *secret.*

Circle S following Half-length Forms. 136. Circle *s* at the end of a half-length form is read after the *t* or *d* indicated by the halving; thus, _ *coat*, _ *coats*; _ *mount*, _ *mounts*; _ *rent*, _ *rents*; _ *rift*, _ *rifts*.

Half-length H. 137. Half-length *h*, when not joined to another stroke, is always written upward; as, _ *height*, _ *heights*; _ *hunt*, _ *hunts*; _ *haft*, _ *hafts*.

Halving Principle not Employed. 138. The halving principle is not employed—

(*a*) In words of more than one syllable when a vowel follows final *t* or *d*, because a final vowel requires a final stroke; as, ⌄ *pit*, but _ *pity*; _ *greed*, but _ *greedy*;

(*b*) When a triphone immediately precedes *t* or *d*; as, _ *fight* but _ *fiat*, _ *died* but _ *diadem*;

(*c*) Where a more distinctive outline is obtained by the use of the stroke *t* or *d*; as, _ *secret*, but _ *sacred*; _ *unavoidable*, but _ *inevitable*; _ *hotly*, but _ *hotel*;

(*d*) Where the half-length *r* [∕] would stand alone, or with final circle *s* only [∕] added; therefore, in such words as _ *right*, _ *rights*, the stroke *t* must be written. The reason for this is to prevent clashing between *rt* and the sign for *and* or *should*, and between *rts* and the sign for *and-is*. Such words as _ *rents*, _ *rifts*, are safely written with a half-length form.

Position of Half-length Forms. 139. Upward or downward half-length characters must not be written through the line for the indication of vowels. Where the first upstroke or the first downstroke in an outline is a half-length, the outline is written so that the half-length stroke appears over the line for the indication of a first-place vowel, and on the line for the indication of a second or a third-place vowel; thus, ⌐⌐⌐ *optical,* ⌐ *vertical,* ⌐⌐⌐ *lightly,* ⌐ *lately,* ⌐⌐ *witness,* ⌐⌐ *military,* ⌐ *netted,* ⌐ *tint.*

Exercise 83

Read, copy, and transcribe

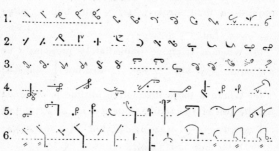

Exercise 84

Write in Shorthand

1. Tie, tight, trite, Coe, coat, coats, Kate, skate.
2. Weigh, weight, weighty, fry, fright, frights.
3. Gray, grade, grades, graded, met, metal.
4. Label, labelled, open, opened, land, lands, lent.
5. Tight, tied, tidy, wit, witty, pat, patty.
6. Heat, heats, hunt, hunts, raid, raids.

GRAMMALOGUES

___ *quite,* __ *could;* ⁔ *accord-ing,* ⌒ *cared:*

⌒ *guard,* ⌒ *great;* ⁔ *called,* ⌒ *equalled, cold;*

⌒ *gold;* ᑦ *that,* ᑕ *without,* ⟋ *wished.*

Exercise 85

Read, copy, and transcribe

Exercise 86

Write in Shorthand

It-has-been maintained *that* certainty does-not admit *of* degrees *of any* kind ; *that-there-can-be* no shade *of difference in-the* intensity *of-our* certainty. *But* let us see.   *A* man may-*be* certain *that-he* settled *his* debt *with-his* tailor *on-the* 10th *of* October, *and-in gold*, or *that-he* paid *his* local rates *on* demand. *But is-this* certainty *equalled* by-*the* certainty *with-which* he knows *that* three *and* four make seven, or *that* heat will melt butter?   *Is there* not *a great difference?*

Summary

1. Halving **a** stroke indicates the addition of *t* or *d*.
2. Unless it is finally hooked, or has an attached diphthong, a light stroke in words of one syllable is halved for *t* only, and a heavy stroke for *d* only.
3. Vowel-signs to halved forms are read next to the primary stroke.
4. Half-length *h*, when not joined to another stroke, is always written upward ; half-length upward *r* must not be written alone, or with a final circle *s* only added.
5. The halving principle is not applied when **a** word ends with a vowel, when *t* or *d* is immediately preceded by a triphone, and in a few other cases where the fuller form is necessary to secure distinction of outline.
6. Half-length forms should not be written through the line for vowel indication.

CHAPTER XXIII

THE HALVING PRINCIPLE (Section 2)

Strokes M, N, L, R. 140. (a) The four strokes ⌒ ‿ ⌐ ⟍ which are halved to express the addition of *t*, are also halved and thickened to indicate the addition of *d*; thus, ⌒ *md*, ‿ *nd*, ⌐ *ld* (down), ⟍ *rd*, as in the words ⌒ *mate*, ⌒ *made*; ⋋ *aimed*, ⊥ *timid*; ‿ *neat*, ‿ *need*, ‿ *end*; ⋎ *old*, ⟍ *aired*.

(b) The half-length form ⌐ *ld*, standing alone, is used only for words beginning with a vowel; as, ⌐ *ailed*, ⋎ *old*; so that words like ⌇⌐ *sold*, ⋰⌐ *styled*, ⋎⌐ *holed*, must be written with the full strokes.

(c) When a vowel occurs between *l-d* or between *r-d*, both consonants must be written in full. Compare ⋎⌐ *pallid* with ⟍ *paled*; ⟋ *married* with ⌐⌐ *marred*; ⋎⌐ *sorrowed* with ⟍ *sword*; ⟋ *hurried* with ⋎ *hoard*.

(d) The signs ⌐ ⟍ cannot be halved to represent the syllables *-lerd*, *-rerd* respectively, because the forms ⌐ ⟍ are used for representing *ld*, *rd*, as explained above.

(e) The strokes ⌒ *mp*, *mb*, ‿ *ng* cannot be halved for the addition of either *t* or *d*, unless they are hooked initially or finally; thus, ⌐⌐ *impute*, ⌐ *imbued*, ⟍⌐ *belonged*; but ⌐ *hampered*, ⌐ *rampart*, ⌐⌐ *lingered*, ⋋ *impugned*.

107

RT and LT. 141. (*a*) The signs for *rt* and *lt* are generally written upward; thus, �⌍ *part*, ∨ *pelt*, ⌣ *fort*, ⌣ *fault*; but ⌢ *lt* is written downward after ⌣ *n* and ⌣ *ng*, as in ⌢ *inlet*, ⌢ *ringlet*; and it is written downward after ⌢ *w* if no vowel follows *l*; thus, ⌊ *dwelt*, but ⌊ *twilight*.

(*b*) The light sign ╱ may be used for *rd* when it is not convenient to write ⌐; thus, ⌐ *lard*, ⌐ *coloured*, ⌐ *cordage*, ⌐ *preferred*.

(*c*) After the *shun* hook, ⌐ *st* may be written downward or upward; thus, ⌐ *protectionist*, ⌐ *progressionist*.

Joining of Strokes of Unequal Length. 142. (*a*) The halving principle may be applied to words like ⌐ *afford*, ⌐ *named*, where the difference of thickness shows the inequality of length; but in other cases two strokes of unequal length must not be joined unless there is an angle at the point of junction. Words like ⌐ *cooked*, ⌐ *looked*, ⌐ *propped*, ⌐ *minute*, ⌐ *fact*, must, therefore, be written with full-length strokes.

(*b*) Half-sized *t* or *d* is always disjoined when immediately following the strokes *t* or *d*; thus, ⌐ *attitude*, ⌐ *treated*, ⌐ *dreaded*, ⌐ *credited*. The half-sized stroke is also disjoined in some other cases, as ⌐ *aptness*, ⌐ *tightness*, ⌐ *hesitatingly*.

Past Tenses. 143. In past tenses *-ted* or *-ded* is always indicated by half-length *t* or *d* respectively; thus, ⌐ *parted*, ⌐ *braided*, ⌐ *coated*, ⌐ *graded*.

The Halving Principle in Phraseography.   144. The halving principle is employed in phraseography as follows—

(a) For the word *it*, as in ⌣ *if it*, ⌣ *if it is* ; (b) *not*, as in ⌐ *I am not*, ⌒ *you may not*, ⌐ *I will not* ;   (c) *word* and *would* by ⌒ as in ⌐ *this word*, ⌒ *we would be* ; and (d) in phrases like ⌐ *at all times*, ⌒ *able to make*.

Exercise 87

Read, copy, and transcribe

1.

2.

3.

4.

5.

6.

Exercise 88

Write in Shorthand

1. Amid, signed, doled, dazzled, sailed, heard.
2. Collide, colt, borrowed, bored, thronged.
3. Impede, dreamed, scampered, conquered.
4. Quilt, quilled, sunlight, answered, glared.
5. Chatted, treated, pathetic, flared, deadness.
6. Liken, likened, exported, shunted, trended.

GRAMMALOGUES

cannot; *gentleman*, *gentlemen*; *particular*, *opportunity*; *child*; *build-ing*; *told*; *tried*, *trade, toward, towards*; *hand, under*.

Exercise 89

Read, copy, and transcribe

Exercise 90

Write in Shorthand

Quite early *in* man's attempt *to* penetrate *into-the great* secrets *of-the* earth, *when-he tried to*-find *its* hidden treasures *of gold and* diamonds *for-the* purposes *of-trade*, he learned one *important* fact, namely,

that-it grows hotter *as you* descend. *This-is* evident,
also, *from-the* hot springs found *in different* parts *of-
the* world, *and* still *more* evident *from-the* volcanoes
which, *when* violently active, pour out molten rock
until *it* covers *the* country around *to a* thickness *of-*
many feet. *A great* authority *on-the subject has*
asserted *that-there-are* slight earth tremors every
quarter *of an hour*. *The hand of-*man seems weak
indeed *when-we-think of-the* wondrous power *of-*these
mighty forces.

Summary

1. The four strokes ⌒ ⌣ (⌐ are halved and
   thickened for the addition of *d*.
2. The thickened forms ⌐ ⌐ are not used if **a**
   vowel comes between *l-d*, *r-d*.
3. *Ler* and *rer* are never halved ; *mp* and *ng*
   may be halved when initially or finally
   hooked.
4. *Rt* is generally written upward ; *lt* is written
   upward, except after *n*, *ng* ; after *w*, *lt* is
   written downward if no vowel follows *l*.
5. The upward form ⟋ may be used medially and
   finally for *rd*.
6. The half-length) *st* may be written downward or upward after *shun*.
7. Two strokes of unequal length must not be
   joined unless there is an angle at the point
   of junction, or unless, in the case of curves,
   the difference of thickness clearly shows the
   inequality of length.
8. Half-sized *t* or *d* is always disjoined when
   immediately following the strokes *t* or *d*.
9. In past tenses *-ted* or *-ded* is always indicated
   by half-length *t* or *d* respectively.
10. The halving principle is used in phraseography
    to represent *it, not, word, would*.

CHAPTER XXIV

THE DOUBLING PRINCIPLE

The General Rule. 145. With the few exceptions named below, the addition of the syllable -*tr* or -*dr*, or -THr, or, in common words -*ture*, is indicated by doubling the length of the preceding stroke; thus,

⌵‥ *fie,* ⌵ *fighter;* │ *ten,* │ *tender;* ‥‥ *nigh,*

⁀‥ *neither;* └ *track,* └ *tractor;* ⌒ *seek,*

⌒‥ *sector;* ⊥ *Dow,* │ *doubler;* ⟋ *won,*

⟋ *wonder;* ⌒ *grave,* ⌐‥ *grafter;* ⟋ *impugn,*

⌒ *impounder;* ⌣ *centre,* ⟍ *central;*

⌣ *enter,* ⌣⁀ *enteric;* ⟍‥ *pick,* ⟍‥ *picture;*

⌁‥ *few,* ⎸ *future,* ⌣ *nay,* ⌣ *nature;* ‥‥ *natural.*

Doubling of Straight Strokes. 146. The doubling principle must not be applied to a straight stroke unless it follows a circle or stroke consonant, or has a final hook, or an attached diphthong. Compare

⌒‥ *skater* with ⌐⎸ *cater;* ⟍ *captor* with ⟍ *potter;*

⟋ *wonder* with ⟋ *wader;* │ *doubler* with

⌐ *daughter;* │ *tutor* with ⟨ *tether.*

Strokes MP and NG. 147. The character ⌒ *mp-mb,* when not initially hooked, is doubled for the addition of -*er*, and the character ⌣ *ng* for the addition of -*kr*, -*gr*; thus, ⟍ *bump,* ⟍ *bumper;* ⟍ *vamp,* ⟍ *vamper;* ⌣ *inker,* ⌣ *linger,* ⌣ *Ingersoll.*

112

Alternatives for MPR, MBR. 148. There are therefore alternative forms for *mpr*, *mbr*, the double-length form ⌒ and the hooked form ⌒ The hooked form is used when *mpr*, *mbr* immediately follows an upstroke or — *k* ; in all other cases the double-length form is used ; thus, ⌒ *umber*, but ⌒ *slumber;* ⌐ *tamper*, but ⌐ *hamper ;* ⌐ *chamber,* but ⌐ *cumber.*

Alternatives for NG-KR, NG-GR. 149. There are alternative forms for *ng-kr*, *ng-gr*, the double-length ⌣ and the hooked form ⌣ The double-length form is used initially and when following a circle or an upstroke. In all other cases, the hooked form is written ; thus, ⌐ *anchorage*, but ⌐ *bunkering;* ⌣ *sinker*, but ⌐ *drinker ;* ⌐ *hunger*, but ⌐ *pinker ;* ⌐ *rancour*, but ⌐ *canker.*

Stroke L. 150. The stroke *l*, standing alone, or with only a final circle attached, is doubled for *-tr* only ; thus, ⌐ *letter*, ⌐ *letters ;* ⌐ *alter*, ⌐ *alters ;* but ⌐ *leader*, ⌐ *leather.*

Circle S and Double-length Strokes. 151. Circle *s* at the end of a double-length form is read after the syllable indicated by doubling ; thus, ⌐ *voters*, ⌐ *renders*, ⌐ *rafters*, ⌐ *rectors*, ⌐ *pictures.*

Past Tenses. 152. When the present tense of a
verb of more than one syllable is written with either
a double-length character or a hooked form, the past
tense is written with the halving principle; thus,

⟍ *ponder,* ⟍ *pondered ;* ‾‾ *canter,* ⟍ *cantered ;*

⟋ *winter,* ⟋ *wintered ;* ‾‾ *matter,* ⟍ *mattered ;*

⟋ *malinger,* ⟋ *malingered ;* ‾‾ *conquer,*

‾‾ *conquered.*

Doubling Principle not employed. 153. The
doubling principle is not employed—

(*a*) When a vowel follows final *-tr, -dr,* etc., because
a final vowel requires a final stroke for the vowel
sign ; as, ⟨ *flatter,* but ⟨ *flattery ;* ⟋ *winter,*
but ⟋ *wintry ;* ⟨ *feather,* but ⟨ *feathery ;*
‾‾ *anger,* but ‾‾ *angry.*

(*b*) In words like ⟋ *panther,* ⟍ *Arthur,* where
the *thr* is a light sound.

Position of Double-length Strokes. 154. (*a*) All
double-length downstrokes are written through the
line ; as, ⟍ *painter,* ⟨ *fetter,* │ *tender.*

(*b*) Double-length horizontals are written either
above the line or on the line, according to the first
vowel heard in the word ; thus, ‾‾ *matter,*
⟋ *mother,* ⟋ *enter,* ‾‾ *neither.*

(*c*) Double-length upstrokes are written *above,*
or *on,* or *through* the line, according to the first vowel
heard in the word ; thus, ⟋ *loiter,* ⟋ *render,*
⟋ *hinder.*

The Doubling Principle in Phraseography. 155. The doubling principle is employed in phraseography for the indication of the words *their*, *there*; thus, ⌒ *in*, ⌒ *in their*; ⌒ *I know*, ⌒ *I know there is*; ⌐ *take*, ⌐ *take their way*; ＼ *I can be*, *I can be there*; ⟋ *has to be*, ＼ *has to be there*; ⟍ *upon*, ＼ *upon their*.

Exercise 91

Read, copy, and transcribe

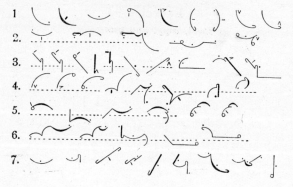

Exercise 92

Write in Shorthand

1. Flatter, thither, aster, voters, enters, neuter.
2. Fender, lavender, shedder, feeders, godfathers.
3. Central, centralization, dysenteric, eccentric.
4. Bidder, spider, plotter, sector, painter, winter.

5. Louder, Lowther, builder, cylinder, chambermaid, sinker, hunger, hungered, whimper, conquer.
6. Mutter, muttered, wander, wandered, temper, tempered, alter, altered, shatter, shattered.
7. Pander, pantry, seconder, secondary, voter, votary, cinder, cindery, enter, entry.

GRAMMALOGUES

chaired, *cheered*; *sent*; *third*, *short*; *spirit*; *yard*, *word*; *rather*, *writer*; *wonderful-ly*; *therefore*; *school*, *schooled*.

Exercise 93

Read, copy, and transcribe

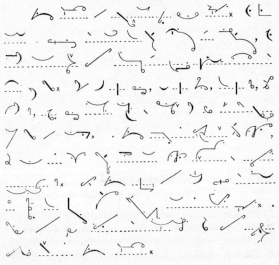

Exercise 94

Write in Shorthand

We-have to *hand* to-day, *under* last Wednesday's date, another copy *of-the wonderful* catalogue issued by Crowder *and* Sanderson.   *Their* motor cycle department *rather* appeals *to-the* boys *in-this school, and-we-have, therefore, sent word that-we should* like *several* extra copies *of-the* catalogue. *The* new leather belt, just *over a yard in* length, *for* use *with a* water-proof coat, seems *wonderfully* cheap.   *There-is,* also, *a rather* attractive lamp, *with* silvered reflector, suitable *for any* holder, *and-this should* take well *with-the* boys.   These *people are* enterprising.   *They-are* inventors *as*-well-*as* dealers, *and-therefore we should-be*-able-*to* rely upon-*their* motor fittings *being* absolutely up *to* date.

Summary

-*tr*, -*dr* or -THr, or, in common words, -*ture* is added	by doubling the length of the preceding stroke.
-*er* is added to the curve ⌒, and -*kr* or -*gr* is added to the curve ⌣	by doubling the length of the curve.
there or *their* in a phrase is expressed	by doubling the length of the preceding stroke.

Past tenses of verbs of more than one syllable.	are written with the halving principle.
The Doubling Principle is not applied	when a final vowel immediately follows *-tr*, *-dr*, etc.
The double-length form ⌒ *-mpr* or *-mbr*	is written (*a*) initially ; (*b*) after a circle or loop ; (*c*) after a downstroke.
The hooked form ⌒ *-mpr* or *-mbr*	is written in all other cases.
The double-length form ⌣ *ng-kr* or *ng-gr*.	is written initially and when following a circle or an upstroke.
The hooked form ⌣ *ng-kr* or *ng-gr*.	is written in all other cases.

CHAPTER XXV

DIPHONIC OR TWO-VOWEL SIGNS

In many words two vowels occur consecutively, each being separately pronounced. To represent these, special signs have been provided called *diphones* (from the Greek *di* = double, and *phōnē* = a sound).

Use of Diphones. 156. In most instances, the first of the two consecutive vowels is the more important, and therefore the diphonic sign is written in the vowel-place which the first vowel would take if this occurred alone. The method of using the *diphones* is explained in the following rules.

157. The *diphone* ⌐ is written as follows—

(*a*) In the first vowel-place to represent the vowel *ah* or *ă* and any vowel immediately following; thus, ⟍ sah*i*b, ⌐ Jud*ai*sm.

(*b*) In the second vowel-place to represent *ā* or *ĕ*, and any vowel immediately following; thus, ⟍ l*ay*er, ⟍ l*ai*ty, ⟍ betr*ay*al, ⟍ surv*eyo*r;

(*c*) In the third vowel-place to represent *ē* or *ĭ* and any vowel immediately following; thus, ⟍ r*ea*l, ⟍ r*ea*lity, ⟍ r*e-e*nter, ⟍ am*ia*ble, ⟍ m*ea*nder, ⟍ g*eo*graphy, ⟍ g*eo*graphical, ⟍ champ*io*n, ⟍ heav*ie*st, ⟍ bur*yi*ng, ⟍ glor*io*us, ⟍ cr*ea*tor, ⟍ cr*ea*tion, ⟍ ser*ia*l, ⟍ ser*io*us.

158. The *diphone* ⌐ is written as follows—

(*a*) In the first vowel-place to represent *aw* and any vowel immediately following; thus, ⌐ *flawy*, ⌐ *drawer*, ⌐ *drawings*, ⌐ *cawing*;

(*b*) In the second vowel-place to represent ō and any vowel immediately following; thus, ⌐ *showy*, ⌐ *bestowal*, ⌐ *poet*, ⌐ *poetical*, ⌐ *coercion*, ⌐ *coincide*, ⌐ *coincident*, ⌐ *heroic*.

(*c*) In the third vowel-place to represent ōō and any vowel immediately following; thus, ⌐ *bruin*, ⌐ *brewery*, ⌐ *Louisa*, ⌐ *Lewis*, ⌐ *truant*, ⌐ *Druid*, ⌐ *Druidical*, ⌐ *shoeing*, ⌐ *hallooing*.

Extended Use of Angular Sign. 159. The angular sign ∠ is also used to represent the consecutive vowels in the small class of words like ⌐ *Spaniard*, ⌐ *million*, ⌐ *bullion*, ⌐ *question*.

Exercise 95
Read, copy, and transcribe

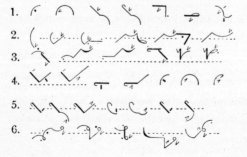

Exercise 96

Write in Shorthand

1. Slay, slayer, bay, bayonet, air, aerometer.
2. Pay, payable, betray, betrayer, obey, abeyance.
3. Re, real, really, reinforce, readdress, readmission.
4. Billow, billowy, blow, blower, co, coincide.
5. Hero, heroic, snow, snowy, slow, slowest.
6. Cruel, brewing, jewel, ruinous, ruination.

Exercise 97

Read, copy, and transcribe

Exercise 98

Write in Shorthand

Dear Mr. Brewer,

It-is to be regretted that-the arrangement with-the band of-the Cleopatra has fallen through, but I-shall-be-able-to re-arrange-the programme and it-will-not affect-the gaiety of-the members of-the

Lyceum *on*-Monday.   *We-have-had* *to*-reappoint *the* late manager *of-the* local theatre *as* Master *of* Ceremonies, *because-he* knows *the* ceremonial *to be* observed, *and-we-shall-have* to reassemble-*the members of-the* chorus, *and* readmit *those-who* retired last June. I-am worrying-*the* decorators, *and* d*o*ing my ut*most to*-make these slowest *of* slow *people* finish *their* work.

> *Very*-truly-*yours*,

Summary

Place	Value of the Diphone ⟋	Place	Value of the Diphone ⟍
1	*ah* or *ă* + any vowel	1	*aw* + any vowel
2	*ā* or *ĕ* ditto	2	*ō* ditto
3	*ē* or *ĭ* ditto	3	*ōō* ditto

The angular sign ⟋ is also used to represent the consecutive vowels in such words as mill*io*n.

CHAPTER XXVI

MEDIAL SEMICIRCLE

As explained in a previous chapter, a right semicircle is used initially as an abbreviation for *w* before the strokes *k, g, m* (and *mp*) and the two forms of *r*. The medial use of a semicircle is explained in the present chapter.

Left and Right Semicircles. 160. (*a*) A *left* semicircle is written in the middle of a word to represent the sounds *wah, wā, wē,* or their corresponding short sounds.

(*b*) A *right* semicircle is written in the middle of a word to represent the sounds *waw, wō, wōō,* or their corresponding short sounds.

161. The following diagram shows the places of the semicircles, and the sounds they represent.

Place	Left Semicircle (	Place	Right Semicircle)
1	represents $w + ah$ or $\breve{a}$	1	represents $w + aw$ or $\breve{o}$
2	,, ,, $+ \bar{a}$,, $\breve{e}$	2	,, ,, $+ \bar{o}$,, $\breve{u}$
3	,, ,, $+ \bar{e}$,, i	3	,, ,, $+ \bar{oo}$,, $\breve{oo}$

162. The medial semicircle is, therefore, simply an abbreviation for *w* followed by a vowel. The sign is usefully written in words like ⌐ *boudoir,* ⌐ *assuage,* ⌐ *sea-weed ;* ⌐ *seaward,* ⌐ *Wordsworth,* ⌐ *lamb's-wool,* i.e. where the *w* is not essential to the outline.

123

Exercise 99

Read, copy, and transcribe

Exercise 100

Write in Shorthand

1. Sealing-wax, twenty, twentieth, Cromwell, Bothwell.
2. Dwindle, dwindled, wherewith, *there*with, bewilder, bewildered.
3. Breakwater, blameworthy, seaworthy, Wandsworth, Cornwallis.
4. Wick, wicked, wickedly, weaken, weakness.

Exercise 101

Read, copy, and transcribe

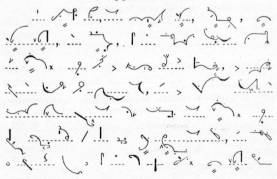

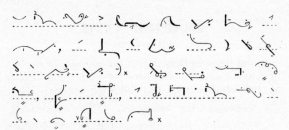

Exercise 102

Write in Shorthand

Dear-Sirs,

We-thank-you for-your-letter *of*-last week *and
we-are* asking Messrs. Cromwell *and* Warbeck, *of*
Wentworth, *to*-look *into-the* matter forthwith. *We*
hope *that-the* flow *of*-water *into-the* workings may
dwindle away *with-the* advent *of-the* dry weather,
and-that-the trouble may cease *of-itself. In-any*-
case, *you*-may-rely upon-us *to-do all-that-we-can* to
stop-*the* nuisance *in*-question. *We-have* already told
our engineer, *Mr.* Walter Welson, *to*-make close
enquiry *into-the* matter, *and-we-thank-you* again
for-the kindly way *in-which-you have* warned us *of-the*
possible loss both *to-ourselves and to-you.*

Yours-truly.

Summary

1. A semicircle is employed medially as an alternative
   to the stroke *w*.
2. A medial *left* semicircle represents *wah, wā, wē,*
   or the corresponding short sounds.
3. A medial *right* semicircle represents *waw, wō,
   wōō,* or the corresponding short sounds.

CHAPTER XXVII

PREFIXES

Initial Com- or Con-. 163. Initial *com-* (or *comm-*) or *con-* (or *conn-*) is expressed by a light dot written at the beginning of the following stroke ; thus, ⟍ *combine,* ⟋ *commence,* ⟋ *congratulate,* ⟋ *connection.* In a few words clearer outlines are obtained by writing the prefixes fully ; thus, ⟋ *commotion,* ⟋ *commission,* ⟋ *commiserate,* ⟋ *consul,* ⟋ *connote.*

In words beginning with the prefix *com-* or *con-*, represented by a dot, the position of the outline is governed by the first vowel after the prefix.

Medial Com-, etc. 164. Medial *com-, con-, cum-,* or *cog-,* either in a word or in a phrase, is indicated by disjoining the form immediately following the *com-,* etc. ; thus, ⟍ *becomingly,* ⟋ *welcoming,* ⟋ *incompetent,* ⟋ *uncontrolled,* ⟋ *circumference,* ⟋ *recognize,* ⟋ *in compliance,* ⟍ *by consent,* ⟋ *I am compelled.* This method may be used after a dash logogram when this is written upward, but not when it is written downward ; compare ⟋ *on the committee,* ⟋ *of the committee ;* ⟋ *should commence* and ⟍ *to commence.*

Accom-. 165. *Accom-* (or *accommo-*) is represented by —— *k,* joined or disjoined ; thus, ⟋ *accommodation,* ⟋ *accompany.*

Intro-. 166. *Intro-* is expressed by ⟍ *ntr ;* thus, ⟋ *introduce,* ⟋ *introspection.*

126

Magna-, etc. 167. *Magna-, magne-* or *magni-* is expressed by a disjoined ⌒ *m ;* thus, ⌢ *magnanimity,* ⌒ *magnetize,* ⌒ *magnify.*

Trans-. 168. *Trans-* may be contracted by omitting the *n ;* thus, ⌐ *transfer,* ⌐ *transmit,* ⌐ *transgression ;* but sometimes the full outline is preferable, as, ⌐ *transcend,* ⌐ *transit.*

Self- and Self-con- or Self-com-. 169. (*a*) *Self-* is represented by a disjoined circle *s* written close to the following stroke in the second vowel-place ; thus, ⌒ *self-defence,* ⌒ *self-made.*

(*b*) *Self-con-* or *self-com-* is indicated by a disjoined circle *s* written in the position of the *con-* dot ; thus, ⌒ *self-control,* ⌒ *self-complacency.*

In- before Str, Skr and H (up). 170. *In-* before the circled strokes ⌐ ⌐ ⌐ is expressed by a small hook written in the same direction as the circle ; thus, ⌐ *instrument,* ⌐ *inscriber,* ⌐ *inhabit.*

Negative Words. 171. (*a*) The small hook for *in-* is never used in negative words, that is, where *in-* signifies *not.* In such cases *in-* must be written with the stroke *n ;* thus, ⌐ *hospitable,* ⌐ *inhospitable ;* ⌐ *scrupulous,* ⌐ *unscrupulous ;* ⌐ *humanity,* ⌐ *inhumanity.*

(b) Words which have the prefix *il-, im-, in-, ir-, un-*, are written in accordance with the following rules, so as to provide the necessary distinction between positive and negative words, and other pairs of words where distinction is required—

(c) By writing the downward *r* or *l* when the rules for writing initial *r* or *l* permit of this being done ; thus, ⟋ *resolute*, ⟍ *irresolute ;* ⟋ *resistible,* ⟍ *irresistible ;* ⟋ *limitable,* ⟋ *illimitable.*

(d) By repeating the *l, m, n* or *r* in cases where a distinction cannot otherwise be obtained ; thus, ⟋ *legal,* ⟋ *illegal ;* ⟋ *mortal,* ⟋ *immortal ;* ⟋ *noxious,* ⟋ *innoxious ;* ⟋ *necessary,* ⟋ *unnecessary ;* ⟋ *redeemable,* ⟋ *irredeemable ;* ⟋ *radiance,* ⟋ *irradiance.*

Logograms. 172. Logograms, joined or disjoined, may be used as prefixes or suffixes ; thus, ⟋ *almost,* ⟋ *understand,* ⟋ *undermine,* ⟋ *unimportant.*

Exercise 103

Read, copy, and transcribe

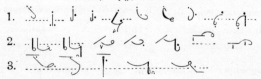

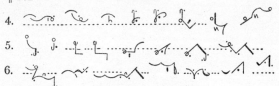

4. ....

5. ....

6. ....

Exercise 104

Write in Shorthand

1. Competent, combat, common, compensate, compound, compact, compare.
2. Conductor, conflict, constant, convulsion, conserve, conscientious, contango.
3. Commissioners, incomplete, recognized, uncongenial, reconsider, incumbent.
4. *We*-were compelled, accompanying, accomplices, introducing, introduces.
5. Magnificent, magnifier, magnificence, transmission, translated, transmitter.
6. Self-possession, self-congratulation, instructor, inherent, inhumanly, insuperable.
7. Illiberal, immaterial, innocuous, unknown, reparable, irreparable, reclaimable, irreclaimable, *under*stood, *under*sell, *trade*-mark.

GRAMMALOGUES

꓿ *selfish-ness* ; ꓾ *inscribe-d* ; ꓾ *inscription* ; ꓿ *instruction* ; ꓿ *instructive*.

Exercise 105

Read, copy, and transcribe

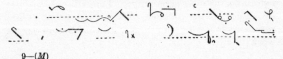

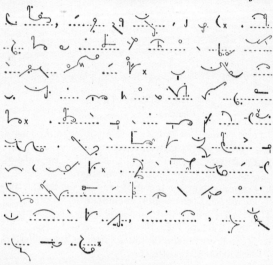

Exercise 106

Write in Shorthand

We-thank-you for-your communication *and instruc-tion* regarding-*the* lightning conductors *for-the* new Conservative Club *in* Conway Road. *The* slight mis-conception *has*-now *been* removed, *and your* recom-mendations *shall-be* carefully considered. *We-are having-the* corner-stones *inscribed this* week, *and-we-have*-no-doubt *that-you*-will-find-*the inscription* will satisfy *you*. *We* suggest *for-your* consideration *that-it-would-be instructive and* useful *to-have a* trans-lation *of-the* Latin *inscription* printed *and* circulated before-*the* opening ceremony. *You*-will-not consider us *selfish* if-*we* arrange *for a* photograph *of-the* ceremony showing *our* name *as* contractors *for-the* work.

Summary

PREFIX	REPRESENTED BY
Initial *con-*, *com-*	A light dot.
Medial *con-*, *com-*	Disjoining the form immediately following the *con-*, etc.
Accom-	The stroke — *k* joined or disjoined.
Intro-	The double-length ⌣ *ntr.*
Magna-, etc.	Disjoined ⌢ *m.*
Trans-	The sign for *trs*, or by the full form.
Self-	A disjoined circle *s* written in the second vowel-place.
Self-con-	A disjoined circle *s* written in the place of the *con-* dot.
In- before certain circled straight strokes	A small hook written with the Right motion.
Il-, *ir-*	Downward *l* or *r*, or by the repetition of the initial consonant.
im-, *in-*, *un-*	Repeating the ⌢ *m* or ⌣ *n.*
Logograms	May be used as prefixes or suffixes.

CHAPTER XXVIII
SUFFIXES AND TERMINATIONS

-Ing. 173. The stroke ‿ is generally employed in the representation of *-ing*. Where this stroke cannot be written, or, where, if written, an awkward joining would result, a light dot is used to represent the suffix *-ing*. The dot *-ing* is written—

(*a*) After light straight downstrokes and downward *r*, as ＼ *paying*, ⌐ *tying*, ／ *etching*, ⅄ *hoeing*, ⟍ *hearing*, ＜ *spluttering*.

(*b*) After circle *ns*, after *k* and *g* hooked for *f* or *v*, and after an upstroke finally hooked; as, ⟋ *prancing*, ⌐ *coughing*, ⌁ *waning*.

(*c*) After a half-length or a double-length stroke where no angle would be obtained by the use of the stroke ‿ , as ⟍ *brooding*, ⟍ *fidgeting*, ⌢ *matting*, ⟍ *fielding*, ⌒ *muttering*.

(*d*) Generally after a contracted logogram; as, ＼ *remembering*, — *coming*, ⟨ *thanking*; but the stroke ‿ is employed in ⟋ *wishing*, ⌒ *calling*, ‿ *having*, ⟍ *surprising*.

(*e*) The dot *-ing* cannot be used medially; therefore the stroke *ng* is written in *-ingly*; thus, ⌐ *admiring*, but ⌐⟋ *admiringly*; ⌁ *deserving*, but ⟍ *deservingly*.

132

(f) Wherever *-ing* would be represented by a dot, *-ings* is indicated by a dash; thus, / *etchings*, ⌐\ *scrapings*, ⌐ *plottings*, ⌐ *windings*, ⌐ *rinsings*.

-Ality, etc.   174. - *Ality*, *-ility*, *-arity*, *-ority*, *-elty*, and similar terminations are expressed by disjoining the stroke immediately preceding the termination; thus, ⌐ *formality*, ⌐ *barbarity*, ⌐ *novelty*, ⌐ *frivolity*, ⌐ *feasibility*, ⌐ *majority*.

-Logical-ly.   175. - *Logical* and *-logically* are expressed by a disjoined / *j*; thus, ⌐ *genealogical-ly*, ⌐ *mythological-ly*.

-Ment.   176. - *Ment* is, as a rule, expressed by ⌐ *mnt*; thus, ⌐ *sentiment*, ⌐ *agreement*. If this sign does not join easily, however, the contracted form ⌣ may be used; thus, ⌐ *imprisonment*, ⌐ *commencement*, ⌐ *refinement*, ⌐ *preferment*.

-Mental-ly-ity.   177. - *Mental*, *-mentally*, and *-mentality* are expressed by a disjoined ⌐ *mnt*; thus, ⌐ *fundamental-ly*, ⌐ *instrumental-ly-ity*.

-Ly.   178. - *Ly* is expressed by ⌐ *l*, joined or disjoined; thus, ⌐ *chiefly*, ⌐ *friendly*; or the hook *l* is employed; thus, ⌐ *deeply*, ⌐ *positively*.

-Ship.   179. - *Ship* is expressed by a joined or disjoined ⌐ *sh*; thus, ⌐ *friendship*, ⌐ *citizenship*, ⌐ *scholarship*, ⌐ *leadership*.

-Fulness and -lessness or -lousness. 180. (*a*) -*Fulness* is expressed by a disjoined ⌣ *fs* ; thus, usefulness, carefulness, gratefulness.

(*b*) -*Lessness* and -*lousness* are expressed by a disjoined ⌒ *ls* ; thus, heedlessness, hopelessness, sedulousness.

-Ward, -wart, -wort ; -yard. 181. -*Ward, -wart* or -*wort*, and -*yard* are expressed by a half-sized *w* and *y* respectively, as in the words, backward, stalwart, brickyard.

Compound Words. 182. Compounds of *here, there, where*, etc., are written as follows—

	in	on	at	to	of	with
HERE						
THERE						
WHERE						

Exercise 107

Read, copy, and transcribe

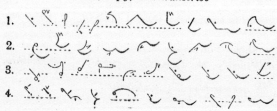

1.
2.
3.
4.

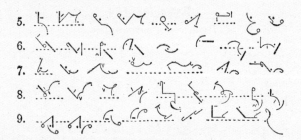

Exercise 108

Write in Shorthand

1. Sapping, tying, teaching, fearing, webbing, wading, lodging, shaking, flogging, loving, scathing, sowing, rushing, slaying, roaring.
2. Dispensing, enhancing, craving, surrounding, ballooning, opposing, menacing, puffing, disjoining, caning, concerning.
3. Pleating, obtruding, permitting, scaffolding, flitting, smothering, dissecting, smelting, sauntering, *speaking*, castings.
4. Solubility, singularity, fatality, novelties, etymological, accompaniment, effacement, sentimentally, vainly, frankly, exhaustively.
5. *Chair*manship, clerkship, playfulness, credulousness, in*difference*, hereby, *there*about, whereunto.

PHRASES

you will be able to,   *we are able to;*
at the same time,   *at some time,*
for some time;   *this was,*   *that was;*
according to the.

Exercise 109

Read, copy, and transcribe

Exercise 110

Write in Shorthand

I-am-sorry *to* interfere *with-the* arrangements *for-the* announcement *of-the* concert season, *but* at-*the-same-time* I-am compelled *to* say *that* I-*think-the* form proposed *is*-not likely *to-have-the* effect *of* introducing new *members to-the* society. I-fear-*the* psychological effect *of-the wording of-the* circular, *which-is* more like *a* command or *instruction* than *an* invitation. I-*think it*-will provoke *a* feeling *of* resentment *in-the*-minds *of-those* whom *you-are* addressing, *and* at-*the*-same-time convey *a* false impression. I-am conscious *of* no *selfishness in* communicating *with-you on-the* matter, *because-it-is quite* immaterial *to-me whether-the member*ship *is large* or small ; *but, as-the* instructor *and* conductor *of-the* choir, I-must, *in* self-defence, warn *the* committee against *a* possible misconstruction *of-their* circular. I-*think-you*-will-*be*-able-*to* induce *them to* change *it.* I-*have-been* wanting *to* see-*you for*-some-time, *and*-if-*you*-will *call* some-time *during-the* coming week I-*shall-be*-glad *of a* little conversation *with-you.*

Revisionary Exercise (C)

I-*cannot quite under*stand *how you*-came *to* act *as you* did *in-the* court *to*-day, *nor how you could put-the* case against *that child with*-such *particular* force, missing no *opportunity that-you*-were able-*to* seize *to*-make-*the* poor *child* appear guilty *of-the* theft. *You*-may say *that, without-the* evidence *of-the gentle-man whose* purse *was*-taken, *and without-the* statements *of-the* other *gentlemen who* said they saw-*the child* put her *hand into-the* old *gentleman's* pocket, *there-would* certainly *have-been* no case *for-the* jury. *But, surely, according-to-the* evidence *of-the guard called* by-*the* defence, *there-was more*-than *a* doubt *that-the* prisoner *was-the child* seen by-*the gentlemen who* testified. *The guard told a* straightforward *tale, and, though-you tried to* shake *his* evidence *you* failed *to do*-so, except *towards-the* end, *when-he* admitted he-saw *a gold* coin drop apparently *from-the child's hands to-the* ground. I-*think-you*-were *a* little *short* with-*the guard,* and I-*was* glad *when-the* people *in-the* court *cheered his* final reply. They *chaired him, too,* at-*the* end *of-the* case, *under* protest by-*him and-his* friends. I-*do*-not *believe-the* poor *child* came out-*of-the*

yard, as stated by-one-*of-your* witnesses, *and*-indeed
I-did-not *believe a word of-that* witness's evidence.
It-was given in a bad *spirit, in a* tone *which sent a*
shiver through everyone *in-the* court. I-know *that*
at-least *a third of-his* story about-*the school and-the
wonderful instruction* he *had* received *there was*
untrue. I-know *this because* I-went to-*the school
myself and you*-will-find my name *inscribed on-the*
roll *of* honour hanging *in-the large* hall. *It-is*-not
wonderful, therefore, that I-*have a* doubt *of-that* man's
word. *It-would-be rather more wonderful* if I-*believed*
his story. I-*think that-he-is a selfish,* vindictive
fellow, *and it-*will-*be instructive* to follow *his* future.
Anyway, I-*shall* set about *an* appeal *for-the child,*
whom I-*believe to be* absolutely innocent *of-the* crime
alleged against her.   (373 words)

Summary

SUFFIX	REPRESENTED BY
-ing	The stroke ⌣ where convenient ; otherwise by a light dot.
-ings	The stroke ⌣ where convenient ; otherwise by a light dash.
-ality, etc.	Disjoining the stroke immediately preceding the termination.
-logical-ly	Disjoining the stroke / *j.*
-ment	The sign ⌐ *mnt,* where convenient ; otherwise by ⌣ *nt.*

-mental-ly-ity	Disjoined ⌒ *mnt.*
-ly	{ The stroke ⌠ *l,* or by a form hooked for *l.*
-ship	The stroke ⌡ *sh.*
-lessness or *-lousness*	{ Disjoined ⌒ *ls.*
-fulness	Disjoined ⌣ *fs.*
-ward, etc., and *yard*	{ Half-sized *w* and *y* respectively.

Compounds	{ Generally formed by joining the outlines for the separate words.

CHAPTER XXIX

CONTRACTIONS

Omission of Consonants. 183. (*a*) Where *p* is very slightly sounded, it may be omitted, as in ⌣ *prompt*, ⌐ *tempt*, ⌐ *assumption*, ⌐ *exemption*; but the *p* is represented in words like ⌐ *trumpet*, ⌐ *trumpeter*, where it is clearly sounded.

(*b*) *K* or *G* is omitted between *ng* and *t*, or between *ng* and *sh*, when no vowel occurs immediately after *k* or *g*; thus, ⌐ *adjun(c)t*, ⌐ *extin(c)tion*. In ⌐ *trinket*, ⌐ *blanket*, and similar words, in which a vowel follows the consonant, the *k* or *g* is retained. The *k* is also retained in past tenses, as ⌐ *inked*, ⌐ *winked*, ⌐ *banked*, ⌐ *linked*.

(*c*) Medial *t*, immediately following circle *s*, may be omitted in many words; thus, ⌐ *postman*, ⌐ *honestly*, ⌐ *tasteful*, ⌐ *mistake*, ⌐ *mistaken*, ⌐ *institute*; and in phrases like ⌐ *most important*, ⌐ *there must be*, ⌐ *your last letter*. In some words, however, the full form is quite as facile as the contracted form; thus, ⌐ *drastic*, ⌐ *elastic*, ⌐ *plastic*.

Exercise 111

Read, copy, and transcribe

1. [shorthand outlines]
2. [shorthand outlines]
3. [shorthand outlines]
4. [shorthand outlines]
5. [shorthand outlines]
6. [shorthand outlines]
7. [shorthand outlines]

Exercise 112

Write in Shorthand

1. Presume, presumptive, bump, bumped, tempt, tempter.

2. Temptation, contempt, contemptible, cramp, cramped, thump, thumped.

3. Consumption, consumptive, stamp, stamped, swamped, resumptive.

4. Indistinct, distinction, extinct, manifest, manifestly, adjustments.

5. Rest, restless, list, listless, dishonest, dishonestly, waste-pipe.

6. Text, textbook, trust, trustworthy, postcard, Post Office.

Exercise 113

Read, copy, and transcribe

Exercise 114

Write in Shorthand

We-are-much-obliged *for-your*-letter *and* estimate *for-the* elastic web. *But surely there*-must-be some mistake *in-your* figures. Please-refer *to-your*-last-letter *to* us, dated 26th October, *in-which-you*-gave us *a* distinctly better price. Manifestly, *the* postponement *of-the*-order *for a* week *cannot* possibly *have*-made so *great a difference in-the*-price. *We* realize *that-the* web *is-the* best-finish, *as-it-is most-important it-should-be, but-you*-must-try *to-improve* upon *your* estimate, or *you-cannot* hope *to-*receive*-the* order. *You*-must-*be* estimating, *we-think, on-the* assumption *that-the* web *is to be* silk finished. *That-is-* not so, *as you*-will-see *on* referring *to-our* last-letter. If-*there-is-to be a* resumption *of* business between-us, *your* estimate will-*have to be* reconsidered. *All-we* ask *for is a* web *with-the* best-finish, *but* not silk, *and of a* tasteful design. *What-can you* offer *to* tempt us *to* pass *the* order *to-you* ?

Other General Contractions.

184. Contractions for a number of words in common use are formed by the omission of a medial or final consonant or syllable. These contracted words, together with the classes of words contracted on the principles explained in the present chapter, constitute what may be termed General Contractions. A prefix or suffix may be attached to a contracted outline, and in this way the list of contractions may easily be extended ; thus,

⌒ *respect,* ⌐ *disrespect,* ⌐⌒ *disrespectful,*

⌒ *respective,* ⌒ *respectively.* The halving principle may be applied to contracted forms for past tenses ; thus, ⌐ *endanger,* ⌐ *endangered ;* but in many cases the same form may safely be employed for both present and past tenses ; thus, ⌒ *respect-ed,* ⌐ *suspect-ed.* Contracted outlines are generally written on the line.

Omission of N

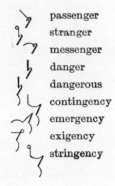

passenger
stranger
messenger
danger
dangerous
contingency
emergency
exigency
stringency

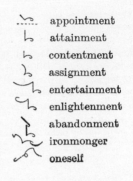

appointment
attainment
contentment
assignment
entertainment
enlightenment
abandonment
ironmonger
oneself

Omission of R

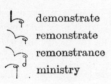

demonstrate
remonstrate
remonstrance
ministry

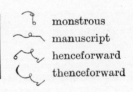

monstrous
manuscript
henceforward
thenceforward

Omission of -ect

expect-ed
inspect-ed-ion
prospect
respect-ed
retrospect

imperfect-ion-ly
suspect-ed
object-ed
project-ed
architect-ure-al

Omission of kt before -ive

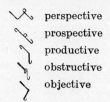

	perspective		destructive
	prospective		destructively
	productive		retrospective
	obstructive		irrespective
	objective		irrespectively

Omission of K before -shun

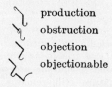

	production		destruction
	obstruction		jurisdiction
	objection		introduction
	objectionable		retrospection

Exercise 115
Write in Shorthand

The appointment of a stranger as Passenger Superintendent is a disappointment to-the local candidates for-the position. There-is a rumour of a demonstration of-protest against what-have-been called the monstrous methods of-the administration in-this-matter. There-is, however, great danger in a form of remonstrance that-may provoke a dangerous outburst in-place of-the-present contentment, and, with great respect to-the leaders, we-fail to see any prospect of-their attaining their object if-they demonstrate in-the way suggested. It-is always the unexpected and unsuspected contingency that-is likely to happen, and-we expect-the present emergency will prove no exception to-the rule. The introduction of a policy of obstruction or destruction, or even of interference with reasonable jurisdiction, may-be productive of discontentment all-round. It-is to be hoped every means will-be sought for-the attainment of-the objective.

Exercise 116

Write in Shorthand

We-fear *there-is*-no *prospect* of success *for-those-who* raise *objection to-the appointment, and, quite irrespective of-the* merits *of-the respective* parties, *we-would* urge-*the abandonment of obstructive* measures *and-the entertainment of-the* suggested resort *to*-threats. Further *enlightenment is* necessary if matters *are to* proceed smoothly *henceforward.* *It-is* pleasant *to*-turn *from this-subject to-the* attractions *of-the* country-side, where *there-are* numerous *objects of entertainment and instruction for all who care to*-look *for-them.* The jerry builder *has*-not-yet begun *his destructive* work, *and-the monstrous things which* he *calls architecture, but which* cause dis*appointment and*-grief *to-the* genuine *architect, have*-not-yet appeared *to-ruin-the prospect.* *The* unspoiled beauty *of* nature still remains *to* compel *our respect*ful admiration, *and to remonstrate in* silence against *those whose object is to*-make money, even *though it* involves *the destruction of-the-most* glorious *prospect.*

Exercise 117

Write in Shorthand

(*a*) Please-send *a messenger to-the passenger* office *and* ask if-*there-is any danger of-the* train *being* late at Macclesfield. *The* present *emergency has* arisen through-*the* death *of-the* man *in*-charge *of-the* post-office, *and-the abandonment of-the stranger's* claim might bring-about-*the very contingency we-are* striving *to*-avoid. *We-had-the* same *emergency on-the appointment of-the* postmaster *three-years*-ago, *and-the enter-tainment* then arranged *had to be* abandoned *because-it-was* felt *that-it-would-be dangerous to* proceed. *The*

abandonment caused dis*appointment*, *of*-course, *but
contentment* followed *enlightenment as-to-the* cause *and*
eventually *the attainment of-the* orginal *object was*
secured.

(*b*) *The demonstration* against *the administration
of-the* local funds *was, in-our-opinion,* a *monstrous*
mistake, *and-we-shall remonstrate as* vigorously *as-
we-can.* The *monstrosity in-the* shape *of an* effigy
of-the chairman of-the administrative committee *was
of-the-most objectionable* nature, *and*-only served *to
demonstrate the* poor taste *of-those-who* designed *it.*
I *should-have to*-write a long *manuscript* if I desired
to-express my resentment properly, *and*-even then
my *remonstrance would-not-be too* strong. I *should*
like *to* assist *in-the administration of*-personal punish-
ment upon-*the* men at-*the* head *of-this monstrous*
business. *It-is* pleasant *to* know *that* no-one *from-the
ministry was* concerned *in-the*-matter.

(*c*) *As-to-the architect's project for-the* alteration
of-the club premises, I *rather suspect that-his* idea
of-the architectural possibilities *is imperfect and*-
incorrect. *With great respect to-him,* because *of-the
imperfection of*-my acquaintance *with architecture,*
I *respect*fully suggest *that-he-should* take counsel *with*
someone *whose architectural* ability *would* entitle
him *to*-express *an opinion.* I *quite expect-the architect*
will consider *me* dis*respect*ful, *and*-I-am upset at-
the prospect of a disagreement *with him.* My *object
is to* secure *an inspection of-the* premises *as* they-*are,
and* I-*believe-that* unexpected *and,* indeed, un*suspected*
possibilities may develop *as a* result. *There-can-be*
no dis*respect in* suggesting *that a retrospective* view *of-
the* case, so-*as-to* secure a proper *perspective, should-be*
under*taken. This-is* exactly *what* I suggested some-
time-ago, *but it-was* considered *an* interference
with-the administration, and no steps were taken.

Exercise 118

Write in Shorthand

Irrespective entirely *of-the different* views *of-the respective* parties *to-the* discussion, I-am compelled *to* consider-*the* possible results *of-the obstructive* course taken by-*the* council.　*There-can-be* no-doubt *that-the objective would-be more* easily attained if-these *merely destructive* methods were abandoned.　They *can* only *be productive* of-mischief *in-the* case of *prospective* candidates *for* admission *to-the* society, *and-this whether we* consider-*the* matter *prospec*tively or *retrospec*tively.　*A retrospective* examination will show *what-has* occurred *in-the* past, *in* similar *circumstances, and a prospective* consideration will show *what-is* likely *to* occur *in-the* future, if-*the respective* parties *are* allowed *to* follow *their-own merely obstructive* ideas.　Each will-*be destructive of-the* other, *and-*will certainly act *destructively*, no matter *what* each may say.　They *should-be* instructed *to* consider, *respec*tively *and* collectively, *the* effects *of-the* present methods *and* advised *to-*refuse *them.*

Exercise 119

Write in Shorthand

The objection to-the obstruction in-the new bill *is-*not simply *a* personal matter.　*The obstruction is objec*tionable *on-several* grounds.　*First, because it-*will certainly lead *to a destruction of-the* opposition *which-has-been* so *care*fully arranged, *and*, secondly, *because-the-*matter *is* one *which* falls *under* another *jurisdiction.　The introduction of* various methods *of-produc*tion *and* reproduction *has* no bearing *on-the* question, *as-the* least *retrospection would-have* shown *beyond* doubt.　*It-*may sound dis*respect*ful, *but* my-*own* view *is that-the architect and-his* friends, *who-are,*

I-*suspect, the* authors *of-the* bill, *are* simply unaware *of-the* real *circumstances of-the* case, *and-have*-not *given-the* project *the* consideration *it* deserves.

Summary

General contractions are formed by the omission of

p   in words where the *p* is only lightly sounded.

k or *g*   between *ng-t* and between *ng-sh.*

t   between circle *s* and a following consonant.

n   in words like   *passenger,*   *emergency,* etc.

r   in words like   *remonstrate,*   *demonstration.*

-*ect*   in words like   *expect-ed,* etc.

-*kt*   in words like   *productive,* etc.

Derivatives are formed from contracted outlines by attaching a prefix or a suffix, as in,   *respect,*   *disrespect,*   *respectively.*

CHAPTER XXX

FIGURES, ETC.

Figures. 185. Figures *one* to *seven*, and the figure *nine* are represented by shorthand outlines. All other numbers, except round numbers, are represented in the ordinary way by the Arabic numerals. In dealing with round numbers the following abbreviations are used :

⌣ *hundred* or *hundredth*, as in 4 400 ;

(or (*thousand* or *thousandth*, as in 3 (3,000 ;

⌐ *hundred thousand*, as in 4(400,000 ;

⌢ *million*, or *millionth*, as in 3 3,000,000 ;

⌣ *hundred million*, as in 7 700,000,000 ;

\ *billion* (a million of millions), as in 4 \ *four billion.*

The principal monetary units are expressed as follows : ⟩ *pounds*, as in 2 £200, 6 (£6,000, 5 ⟩ £5,000,000 ; ⌐ *dollar*, ⌐ *dollars*, as in 15 ($15,000 ; ⟍ *francs*, as in 4⟍ 400 fr. ; ⟋ *rupees*, as in 2⟋ Rs. 2,000,000.

Accent, etc. 186. (*a*) Accent may be shown by writing a small cross close to the vowel of the accented syllable ; thus, ⌐ *ar'rows*, ⌐ *arose'*, ⌐ *renew'.*

150

(*b*) Emphasis is marked by drawing one or more lines underneath; a single line under a single word must be made wave-like, ⌒, to distinguish it from —— *k*.

(*c*) The sign ⪥ indicates that the preceding remark is to be taken humorously.

Proper Names, etc. 187. In the few cases where it is necessary to indicate exactly the vowel following a diphthong, the separate signs should be used and not the triphone as explained in paragraph 35; thus, ⤵ *Bryan*, ⤵ *Bryon*, ⌐| *Myatt*, ⌐| *Myott*, ⌐| *Wyatt*. Similarly, if it is necessary to indicate exactly the second of two consecutive vowels, the separate signs should be used and not the diphone; thus, ⤶ *Leah*, but ⤶ *Leo*; ⌿ *genii*, ⌣ *nuclei*, ⋀ *radii*. The necessity for the use of these separate vowel-signs will be found to arise but seldom.

Scotch, Welsh, and Irish Consonants and Vowels. 188. The Scotch guttural *ch*, and the Irish *gh* are written thus, ⌐ *ch*, as in ⌒ *loch*, ⌒ *Loughrea*, ⌐ *Clogher*. The Welsh *ll* by ⌐ *ll*; thus, ⌒ *Llan*.

Foreign Consonants and Vowels. 189. The German guttural *ch* is written thus, ⌐ *ch*, as in ⌐ *ich*, ⌐ *dach*; French nasal ⌣, as in ⌣ *soupçon*; French and German vowels ⌿ *jeune*, ⌐| *Goethe*, ⌐ *dû*.

Exercise 120

Write in Shorthand

The Chairman, in moving-the adoption of-the report and accounts, dealing first with-the accounts of-the local holding company, said it-would-be noted that-the amount paid up on-the shares was increased by F.42,560, or £3,546 ; this-was to-keep pace with-the increase in capital costs of-the property, including extensions during recent years. Sundry creditors at £3,507 included £2,583 for Java income-tax reserve (of-which £1,666 appearing to-the debit of-profit and loss account was additional for-the-year), besides bonus due to-the staff and-some trade items. The outlay on capital account £3,714, included £2,746 for a new drying installation, smoke house, etc., the balance being for upkeep of-the immature area. They-had now a monthly capacity of 15,000 lb. sheet, the policy of-the board being to increase their output of-this quality to 50 per-cent of-the estate's whole output.

Their cash assets in-London and Java amounted to £16,712, an increase of nearly £5,000. The crop was 449,000 lb., as compared with-the restricted crop of 230,473 lb. in-the preceding year, and against an estimate of 394,000 lb., despite the fact that for-the last two-months of-the-year they-were on a re-stricted basis. The average net selling price was a fraction under 1s. 1d., against 1s. 4·35d. last-year. Thanks, however, to a reduction from 1s. 1·80d. to 8·92d., in-the total costs, the net profit per pound was 4·02d., or 1½d. above-the previous year. It-was largely owing to-this reduction in costs that-they-had made a net profit of £8,843, over 12 per-cent on-the issued capital. He thought-the shareholders would agree that-this-was a pleasing result.

GRAMMALOGUES. *Arranged phonetically*
(*Numbers refer to the position of the ouiline*)

\ 3 put

ᖋ 2 special-ly, 3 speak

\ 3 principle, principal-ly

ᖉ 3 people

ᖈ 1 surprise

ᖈ 1 surprised

⌒ 1 particular, 2 opportu-

⌒ 2 spirit   [nity

\ 2 be, 3 to be

ᖋ 2 subject-ed

ᖋ 2 subjective

ᖋ 2 subjection

ᖈ 1 liberty, 2 member,
    remember-ed, 3 number-ed

\ 3 belief, believe-d

\ 1 behalf

\ 1 been

ᖋ 1 balance

ᖉ 2 build-ing

| 2 it

| 3 itself

ᒋ 2 truth

ᒋ 1 tried, 2 toward, trade

ᒋ 2 towards

ᒋ 2 tell, 3 till

ᒋ 2 told

ᒋ 2 circumstance

ᒋ 2 satisfaction

ᒋ 2 instructive

ᒋ 2 instruction

| 1 had, 2 do, 3 different-
    -ence

ᒋ 1 Dr., 2 dear, 3 during

ᒋ 2 deliver-ed-y

ᒋ 2 deliverance

ᒋ 1 advantage, 3 difficult

/ 1 much, 2 which

ᒉ 2 chair, 3 cheer

ᒉ 1 chaired, 2 cheered

ᒉ 1 child

/ 1 large

ᒉ 1 larger

ᒉ 1 largely

ᒍ 2 general-ly

ᒍ 2 generalization

ᒍ 2 justification

ᒍ 1 gentleman, 2 gentlemen

_ 1 can, 2 come

⌐ 1 because

⌐ 2 care

⌐ 1 accord-ing, 2 cared

⌐ 1 call, 2 equal-ly

⌐ 1 called, 2 equalled, cold

⌐ 2 school

⌐ 2 schooled

− 1 quite, 2 could

⌐ 1 cannot

⌐ 1 inscribe-d

⌐ 1 inscription

_ 1 go, 2 give-n

⌐ 1 signify-ied-ficant

⌐ 1 significance

⌐ 1 signification

⌐ 1 guard, 2 great

⌐ 2 gold

⌐ 1 for

⌐ 2 from

◟ 2 have	⌢ 1 me, 2 him
◟ 2 several	⌢ 1 myself, 2 himself
◟ 1 over, 3 however	⌢ 1 most
◟ 1 valuation	⌢ 1 more, remark-ed,
⌢ 2 very	2 Mr., mere

(1 thank-ed, 2 think	⌢ 1 important-ance,
) 2 third	2 improve-d-ment
	⌢ 1 impossible

(1 though, 2 them	◡ 1 in, any, 3 own
(1 those, thyself, 2 this,	◡ 1 influence
3 thus	◡ 1 influenced, 2 next
(2 themselves	◡ 1 nor, 2 near
) 2 there, their	◡ 2 opinion
(3 within	◡ 1 northern
(2 southern	◡ 1 information
(1 that, 2 without	◡ 1 hand, 2 under
) 3 therefore	◡ 1 sent

◦ 1 has, as, 2 his, is	◡ 1 language, owing.
◦ 2 first	2 thing, 3 young

) 2 was, 3 whose	(2 Lord

) 2 shall, shalt, 3 wish	) 2 your, 3 year
) 2 wished	) 1 yard, 2 word
) 2 selfish-ness	／ 2 are, 3 our, hour
) 3 sure	／ 3 ourselves
) 1 short	／ 2 rather, writer

) 2 usual-ly	◡ 2 we
) 2 pleasure	◡ 2 whether
	／ 2 wonderful-ly

VOWELS	DIPHTHONGS
Dots. ...... a, an, . the; ...... ah !	∧ how;
• aye, eh ?	
Dashes. ...... of, ＼ to; ...... all,	c ...... with, c when; ...... what,
＼ two, too: ...... on, ǀ but ;	
......O, oh ! owe, ǀ he ; ...... and,	ɔ would ;
／ should; ...... awe, ought,	
aught ; ／ who.	∧ ...... beyond, ⌢ you, ∟ ...... why.

GRAMMALOGUES

Arranged alphabetically

a *or* an
accord-ing
advantage
ah !
all
and
any
are
as
aught
awe
aye
balance
be
because
been
behalf
belief-ve-d
beyond
build-ing
but
call
called
can
cannot
care
cared
chair
chaired
cheer
cheered
child
circumstance

cold
come
could
dear
deliver-ed-y
deliverance
difference-t
difficult
do
doctor, Dr.
during
eh ?
equal-ly
equalled
first
for
from
general-ly
generalization
gentleman
gentlemen
give-n
go
gold
great
guard
had
hand
has
have
he
him
himself

his
hour
how
however
importance-ant
impossible
improve-d-ment
in
influence
influenced
information
inscribe-d
inscription
instruction
instructive
is
it
itself
justification
language
large
largely
larger
liberty
Lord
me
member
mere
more
most
Mr.
much
myself

near	should	told
next	significance	too
nor	significant	toward
northern	signification	towards
number-ed	signify-ied	trade
O! oh!	southern	tried
of	speak	truth
on	special-ly	two
opinion	spirit	under
opportunity	subject-ed	usual-ly
ought	subjection	valuation
our	subjective	very
ourselves	sure	was
over	surprise	we
owe	surprised	what
owing	tell	when
own	thank-ed	whether
particular	that	which
people	the	who
pleasure	their	whose
principal-ly	them	why
principle	themselves	wish
put	there	wished
quite	therefore	with
rather	thing	within
remark-ed	think	without
remember-ed	third	wonderful-ly
satisfaction	this	word
school	those	would
schooled	though	writer
selfish-ness	thus	yard
sent	thyself	year
several	till	you
shall, shalt	to	young
short	to be	your

SPECIAL LIST OF CONTRACTIONS

Arranged alphabetically

A

acknowledge

administrator

administratrix

advertise-d-ment

altogether

amalgamate

amalgamation

anything

arbitrary

arbitrate

arbitration

arbitrator

B

bankruptcy

C

capable

certificate

character

characteristic

circumstantial

commercial-ly

cross-examination

cross-examine-d

D

defective

deficient-ly-cy

denomination-al

description

difficulty

discharge-d

distinguish-ed

E

efficient-ly-cy

electric

electrical

electricity

England

English

Englishman

enlarge

enlarger

enthusiastic-iasm

especial-ly

esquire

establish-ed-ment

everything

exchange-d

executive

executor

executrix

expediency

expenditure

expensive

extinguish-ed

F

falsification

familiar-ity

familiarization

familiarize

February

financial-ly

G

govern-ed

government

H

howsoever

I

identical

identification

immediate

imperturbable

incandescence

incandescent

inconsiderate

inconvenience-t-ly

incorporated

independent-ly-ce

indispensable-ly

individual-ly

influential-ly

inform-ed

informer

inspect-ed-ion

insurance

intelligence

intelligent-ly

intelligible-ly

interest

investigation

investment

irrecoverable-ly

irregular

irremovable-ly

irresponsible-ility

J

January

K

knowledge

L

legislative

legislature

M

magnetic-ism
manufacture-d
manufacturer
marconigram
mathematical-ly
mathematician
mathematics
maximum
mechanical-ly
metropolitan
minimum
misfortune
mortgage-d

N

neglect-ed
negligence
never
nevertheless
nothing
notwithstanding
November

O

organization
organize-d
organizer

P

parliamentary
peculiar-ity
perform-ed
performance
performer
perpendicular
practicable
practice
practise-d
prejudice-d-ial-ly
preliminary
probable-ly-ility
proficient-ly-cy
proportion-ed
proportionate-ly
prospectus
public
publication
publish-ed
publisher

Q

questionable-ly

R

ratepayers
recoverable
reform-ed

⌒⌒	reformer	·⌒·	thankful-ly
⌒	regular	⌒	together
⌒	relinquish-ed		**U**
⌒	remarkable-ly	⌒	unanimity
⌒	removable	⌒	unanimous-ly
∧	represent-ed	⌒	uniform-ity-ly
∧	representation	⌒	universal-ly
∧	representative	⌒	universality
∧	republic	⌒	universe
∧	republican	⌒	university
⌒	responsible-ility	·✗·	unprincipled
	S		**W**
⌐	satisfactory	⌒	whatever
⌒	sensible-ly-ility	⌒	whenever
⌒	something	⌒	whensoever
⌒	subscribe-d	⌒	whereinsoever
⌒	subscription	⌒	wheresoever
⌒	substantial-ly	·⌒·	whithersoever
⌒	sufficient-ly-cy		**Y**
⌒	sympathetic	⌒	yesterday
	T		
⌐	telegram		
⌐	telegraphic		

INDEX

The figures refer to the paragraphs, except where the page is mentioned.

THE student is recommended to test his knowledge of the system on reaching this point by entering for the Pitman Theory Certificate. Particulars will be found on the two following pages.

PITMAN'S
SHORTHAND REPORTER

(Being Part 2 of Pitman's Shorthand Instructor.)

NEW ERA EDITION

The above work should be obtained when the student has mastered the Style of Pitman's Shorthand, as presented in this volume. The *Reporter* includes instruction on Note-taking, Transcription, etc. ; Essential Vowels ; Contractions ; Advanced Phraseography ; Business, Political, Banking, Stockbroking, Insurance, Shipping, Electrical and Engineering, Railway, Legal, and Theological Phrases ; Distinguishing Outlines. Comprehensive exercises are furnished throughout, including a large amount of Reading Practice in the Advanced Stage.

Uniform with the " Manual," price 2s. 6d.

PITMAN'S SHORTHAND CERTIFICATES

Third Class (Elementary) for a thorough knowledge of the system up to and including the Halving Principle.

Second Class (Theory) for a thorough knowledge of this book. See form of application opposite.

First Class (Speed) for speeds of 50 words a minute and upwards.

Full Certificate issued to holders of a Second Class Certificate and a First Class for not less than 80 words per minute, certifying to a thorough theoretical and practical knowledge.

Amanuensis Certificate. The candidate is required to take down a Test Passage in Shorthand and type an accurate transcript.

Any of the first three Certificates may be obtained independently of the others. Forms of application postfree from The Examination Department, Phonetic Institute, Bath.

Form of application for Pitman's

THEORY CERTIFICATE

(THEORY—STAGE II)

....19

To the EXAMINATION DEPARTMENT,
Phonetic Institute, Bath

*I enclose for examination a specimen of my writing in
Pitman's Shorthand. If it is found satisfactory, I shall
be glad to receive the* **Certificate of Proficiency in the
Theory of Pitman's Shorthand,** *and to have my success
registered towards the completion of a Full Certificate.*

I send 2s. in payment of the necessary fee.

(*Signed*)   [*Please write distinctly.*]

Name in Full ....
(*Surname to be underlined*)

....

Private Address ....

....

Name in Pitman's Shorthand ....

Name and address of } ....
 Shorthand Teacher } ....

If self-taught, say so ....

Attestation to be signed and dated by the Witness

*I certify that the accompanying specimen of writing signed by me and by
the above applicant, was written in my presence without personal assistance
or reference to books ; that the passage was selected from the newspaper by
myself ; that it was unknown to the applicant ; that it was posted without
alteration ; and that the examination was conducted in conformity with the
rules on page 2 of this form.*

*(*Signed*) ....

Address ....

Date...

Occupation...

* The name and address must be written in longhand.

Directions for applying for a Theory Certificate (Stage II)

1. Every candidate should have a thorough knowledge of Pitman's Shorthand, as presented in *Pitman's Shorthand Manual* (or Chapters I to XXX of the *Shorthand Instructor*); or of the Second *Shorthand Primer*, or Lessons I to XXVIII of the *Commercial Course*, or to the end of the *Rapid Course, the Shorter Course or the School Edition*. Speed in writing is not taken into account as a qualification for this Certificate.

2. The attestor must send, as a proof of the applicant's ability, half a column of current newspaper matter, containing not less than 500 words (to be selected by the attestor) written in Pitman's Shorthand by the candidate. Vowels must be inserted freely to show that the writer understands vocalization. The slip of newspaper, bearing the printed date of issue, must be sent with the specimen of shorthand, as a key. **When two or more candidates apply together, the same test matter should be written by each.** The specimen of shorthand must be the unaided work of the candidate, and written in accordance with the conditions set forth in the attestation clause on the preceding page. The time limit for the examination is two hours.

3. The writing must be done in ink, in the presence of a responsible adult, who is required to see that the examination is conducted in accordance with these rules, and sign the attestation at the foot of the first page of this Form. No teacher of shorthand can act as a witness, nor can a relative of a candidate, or the principal of a school under examination, act in that capacity. No student of a school may act as a witness.

4. Each specimen of writing must be accompanied by a printed Form of Application, and must be addressed to " The Examination Department, Phonetic Institute, Bath," and posted immediately by the attestor, without alteration.

5. The examination fee (2s.) must accompany the application in all cases. Examination fees are not returned under any circumstances, and no reduction is made for second or subsequent applications.

6. Any attempt at dishonest practice will disqualify the applicant, and the fee will be forfeited.

AN ABRIDGED CATALOGUE OF THE
SHORTHAND, TYPEWRITING
AND
STATIONERY PUBLICATIONS
OF
SIR ISAAC PITMAN & SONS, LTD.

LONDON: PITMAN HOUSE, PARKER STREET, KINGSWAY, W.C.2.
BATH: Pitman's Shorthand Institute.
MELBOURNE: Pitman House, Little Collins Street.
Associated Companies:
NEW YORK: Pitman Publishing Corporation, 2 West 45th St.
TORONTO: Sir Isaac Pitman & Sons (Canada), Ltd. (incorporating
The Commercial Text Book Company), Pitman House, 381-383 Church St.
INDIA: A. H. Wheeler and Co., Bombay, Calcutta and Allahabad.

SOLD BY ALL BOOKSELLERS THROUGHOUT THE WORLD

The prices contained in this catalogue apply only to the British Isles.

TERMS—

Cash MUST *be sent with the order,* AND MUST INCLUDE AN APPROXIMATE AMOUNT FOR THE POSTAGE. *When a remittance is in excess of the sum required, the surplus will be returned.*

Sums under 6d. can be sent in stamps. For sums of 6d. and upwards, Postal Orders or Money Orders are preferred to stamps, and should be crossed and made payable to SIR ISAAC PITMAN & SONS, LTD.

Remittances from abroad should be by means of International Money Orders in Foreign Countries, and by British Postal Orders within the British Overseas Dominions. Colonial Postal Orders are not negotiable in England. Foreign stamps CANNOT BE ACCEPTED.

All the Books in this Catalogue are New Era Editions, and in foolscap 8vo size, unless otherwise stated.

SHORTHAND INSTRUCTION BOOKS

PITMAN'S SHORTHAND TEACHER. An elementary work suited for self-instruction or class teaching . . . . **9d.**

Key . . . . **9d.**

PITMAN'S SHORTHAND EXERCISES. A Series of Graduated Sentence Exercises for use with the *Shorthand Teacher* . . **3d.**

PITMAN'S SHORTHAND PRIMERS. For use in Day Schools and Evening Classes. In three Books: Elementary, Intermediate, and Advanced . . . . **Each 9d.**

Keys to Books I, II, and III . . . . . . **Each 9d.**

PITMAN'S SHORTHAND READING LESSONS, No. 1 . . . 8d.
Key . . . 4d.
PITMAN'S SHORTHAND READING LESSONS, No. 2 . . . 8d.
Key . . . 4d.
PITMAN'S SHORTHAND READING LESSONS, No. 3 . . . 8d.
Key . . . 4d.
PITMAN'S SHORTHAND COPY BOOKS, No. 1, 2, 3, and 4
Foolscap 4to (8¾ in. × 6½ in.) . . . . . **Each** 6d.
PROGRESSIVE STUDIES IN PITMAN'S SHORTHAND. A simple and extended exposition of the principles of Pitman's Shorthand . 2/–
PITMAN'S SHORTHAND INSTRUCTOR. Complete Instruction in the system . . . . Cloth 4/6
Key . . . 2/–
Cloth 2/6
SUMMARIES FROM "PITMAN'S SHORTHAND INSTRUCTOR"
Size, 2⅞ in. × 4 in. . . . . 4d.
GRADED SHORTHAND READINGS—
Elementary, with Key. In crown 8vo, oblong . . . 10d.
Intermediate, with Key. In crown 8vo, oblong . . . 10d.
Advanced, with Key. In crown 8vo, oblong . . . 10d.
GRADUATED READING EXERCISES IN PITMAN'S SHORTHAND.
These exercises are taken from *Pitman's Graded Shorthand Readings* (Elementary and Intermediate) 1/–
PITMAN'S SHORTHAND MANUAL. Contains instruction in the Intermediate Style with 120 exercises. Paper . . . 2/6
Cloth 3/–
Key . . . 9d.
SHORTHAND MANUAL READING AND DICTATION EXERCISES 9d.
PITMAN'S SHORTHAND GRADUS. Writing Exercises in ordinary print for *Manual* . . . . 3d.
PITMAN'S SHORTHAND REPORTER. Containing instruction in the Advanced Style, with 52 Exercises 2/–
Cloth 2/6
Key . . . 9d.
REPORTING EXERCISES. Exercises on all the rules and contracted words. In ordinary print, counted for dictation . . . 6d.
Key . . . . In Advanced Style 1/–
PITMAN'S SHORTHAND WRITING EXERCISES AND EXAMINATION TESTS. In ordinary print. In crown 8vo. . . . 2/–
Key. In crown 8vo, cloth 3/6
PROGRESSIVE WRITING AND DICTATION EXERCISES. A collection of 82 letters and narrative exercises taken from the larger work, *Shorthand Writing Exercises and Examination Tests.* In crown 8vo. . . . 1/–
Key . . . 1/6
PROGRESSIVE WORD EXERCISES. Containing exercises selected from the larger work, *Shorthand Writing Exercises and Examination Tests.* In crown 8vo 1/–
Key . . . 1/6
EXERCISES ON THE POSITION RULES OF PITMAN'S SHORTHAND. In crown 8vo 1/–
GRADUATED TESTS IN PITMAN'S SHORTHAND. Illustrating all the rules in the Intermediate Style. In notebook form, post 8vo (6½ in. × 4½ in.), with ruled paper . . . . . 8d.
PITMAN'S SHORTHAND DRILL EXERCISES (8½ in. × 6 in.) . 8d.
PITMAN'S PHRASE DRILL NOTEBOOK (8 in. × 5 in) With Key 6d.
RAPID COURSE IN PITMAN'S SHORTHAND. A series of Twenty Simple Lessons covering the whole of the system. Complete with supplementary exercises. In crown 8vo, cloth . . . 4/6

RAPID COURSE IN PITMAN'S SHORTHAND. Without Appendix

Paper 2/–
Cloth 2/6

Key . 2/–
ADDITIONAL EXERCISES ON "PITMAN'S SHORTHAND RAPID COURSE" . 10d.
READING EXERCISES ON THE RAPID COURSE. Forming the Key to *Additional Exercises on the Rapid Course* . 1/–
RAPID COURSE READING AND DICTATION EXERCISES . . 8d.
RAPID COURSE SHORTHAND READER 1/–
SHORTER COURSE IN PITMAN'S SHORTHAND. A brief course for popular use 1/–
Key . . . . 6d.
ADDITIONAL EXERCISES ON SHORTER COURSE . . 6d.
PITMAN'S SHORTHAND COMMERCIAL COURSE. With Exercises Specially adapted for Commercial Students . Cloth 4/6
Key . . . 2/–
ADDITIONAL EXERCISES FOR "PITMAN'S SHORTHAND COMMERCIAL COURSE" 1/–
PITMAN'S SHORTHAND COMMERCIAL COURSE. Without Exercises 2/6
PITMAN'S SHORTHAND COMMERCIAL COURSE. Notebook and Exercises 2/6
READING EXERCISES ON THE SHORTHAND COMMERCIAL COURSE . 9d.
THE ONE THOUSAND COMMONEST WORDS. Compiled by Dr. LEONARD P. AYRES . . . . 6d.
PITMAN'S SHORTHAND SCHOOL EDITION. For use in day and evening continuation schools. Cloth . . 2/6
Key . 1/–
STUDENTS' SHORTHAND EXERCISES, EXAMINATION GUIDE, AND SPEED TESTS. By A. FIELDHOUSE, F.R.S.A., and E. E. FIELDHOUSE, M.A., LL.B. Crown 8vo., cloth . 3/–
ALKS WITH SHORTHAND STUDENTS. By JAMES HYNES . 2/–
CHATS ABOUT PITMAN'S SHORTHAND. By GEORGE BLETCHER . 2/–
LECTURETTES ON PITMAN'S SHORTHAND. By JAMES HYNES . 2/–
FACILITY EXERCISES FOR SHORTHAND STUDENTS. By JAMES HYNES . . . . . 4d.
PITMAN'S SHORTHAND CATECHISM. Containing over 1,200 questions and answers on the theory of the system. In crown 8vo 2/–
EXAMINATION NOTES ON PITMAN'S SHORTHAND. By H. W. B. WILSON. Crown 8vo, cloth . . 2/–
WORD AND PHRASE-BUILDING EXERCISES IN PITMAN'S SHORTHAND. By JAMES HYNES . . . 9d.

GRAMMALOGUES AND CONTRACTIONS

DICTATION TESTS ON THE GRAMMALOGUES AND CONTRACTIONS OF PITMAN'S SHORTHAND. By D. J. GEORGE . 1/–
GRAMMALOGUES AND CONTRACTIONS. For use in classes. 3d.
VEST POCKET LIST OF GRAMMALOGUES AND CONTRACTIONS OF PITMAN'S SHORTHAND. Size 2⅜ in. × 1¾ in. . 3d.
HOW TO PRACTISE AND MEMORIZE THE GRAMMALOGUES OF PITMAN'S SHORTHAND. Compiled by D. J. GEORGE. Size 7¾ in. × 5 in. . . . . 6d.
GRAMMALOGUE CHARTS. Size 23 in. × 36 in. . . 2/6
REVISION EXERCISES ON THE GRAMMALOGUES AND PHRASE WRITING. By JAMES HYNES . . . 8d.

SHORTHAND DICTIONARIES

PITMAN'S SHORTHAND DICTIONARY. Contains the shorthand forms, fully vocalized, for 62,000 words. Crown 8vo . Cloth **7/6**

PITMAN'S POCKET SHORTHAND DICTIONARY. Royal 32mo (3⅛ in. × 4¾ in.) . . . . Cloth **2/6**
Leather **3/6**

PITMAN'S ENGLISH AND SHORTHAND DICTIONARY. Edited by A. REYNOLDS, M.A. Contains concise definitions as well as shorthand forms. Crown 8vo. **10/–**

SHORTHAND PHRASE BOOKS, ETC.

SHORTHAND WRITERS' PHRASE BOOK AND GUIDE. Each includes about 1,500 Technical Terms and Phrases with Shorthand equivalents. Each in fcap. 8vo, about 92 pp. **2/–**

Banking	Legal
Commercial	Railway
Insurance	Electrical and Engineering

PHONOGRAPHIC PHRASE BOOK. Over 2,400 useful general Phrases **1/6**
Cloth **2/–**

REPORTERS' PHRASE BOOK. By K. S. AIYAR, B.A. Contains a valuable list of phrases and "short-cuts." In crown 8vo. . **2/–**

MEDICAL REPORTING IN PITMAN'S SHORTHAND. By H. DICKINSON. With an Introduction and Lists of Phraseograms, Outlines, and Abbreviations. In crown 8vo, cloth . . **3/6**

TECHNICAL REPORTING. By THOMAS ALLEN REED . . **3/6**

POLICE PHRASE BOOK AND VOCABULARY . . . **1/–**

CIVIL SERVICE SHORTHAND WRITER'S PHRASE BOOK. Compiled by A. MARSHALL, P.C.T. **2/–**

MOTOR TRADE PHRASE BOOK AND VOCABULARY . **1/–**

ABASCRIPT. By G. P. LELY. For writing figures, sums of money, etc., at voice speed. Size 6 in. by 9 in. 40 pp. . . . **3/–**

JAB FIGURES. By G. P. LELY. A useful book for Pitman Shorthand Writers, representing in an abbreviated manner, telephone and car numbers, Sizes 6½ in. by 4½ in. . . . . . **6d.**

DICTATION AND SPEED PRACTICE BOOKS

GRADED LITERARY DICTATOR. For theory and elementary speed classes. In crown 8vo, 64 pp. **1/–**

GRADED LITERARY SHORTHAND READER. Forms the key to *Graded Literary Dictator*. In crown 8vo, 90 pp. . . **1/6**

SPECIALIZED CORRESPONDENCE BOOKS. (1) The Chemical Trade. (2) The Paper Trade. In ordinary print . . . Each **6d.**

PRACTICAL DICTATION EXERCISES FOR BEGINNERS. In crown 8vo, 48 pp. . . . . **9d.**

REPORTING PRACTICE. Dictation Exercises in ordinary type, marked in 20's and 30's. In crown 8vo. . . . **3/6**

THE EXPERT DICTATOR. By C. J. SAPHIER, M.C.S., and T. J. SMYTH. In demy 8vo, cloth gilt **5/–**

PROGRESSIVE DICTATOR. Letters in ordinary print. Counted for various rates of speed. In crown 8vo, cloth . . . **2/6**

DICTATION PRACTICE IN BUSINESS CORRESPONDENCE. A collection of business letters relating to various trades and professions. In crown 8vo **1/–**

GUIDE TO HIGH SPEED WRITING IN PITMAN'S SHORTHAND. By
EMILY D. SMITH, F.C.T.S., and A. JEFFREY MUNRO, F.C.T.S. In
crown 8vo . . . . Cloth   **2/6**

SHORTHAND CANDIDATE'S DICTATION EXERCISES. Nos. 1 and 11.
In crown 8vo. . . . . **Each**   **2/-**

BUSINESS LETTERS FOR DICTATION. In crown 8vo, cloth .   **3/6**
Key in Shorthand **3/6**

GRADUATED COMMERCIAL LETTERS FOR DICTATION . . **8d.**

EXERCISES IN LETTER WRITING IN PITMAN'S SHORTHAND. By
A. H. GILBERTSON, A.C.I.S. 7⅜ in. by 5⅛ in. **1/-**

TESTS FOR SPEED STUDENTS. In crown 8vo **2/-**

SPEED TESTS AND GUIDE TO RAPID WRITING IN SHORTHAND.
In crown 8vo. **2/6**

ELEMENTARY EXAMINATION SPEED TESTS. In crown 8vo. . **8d.**

FIVE-MINUTE SPEED TESTS (Second Series). The speeds range from
80-160 words a minute. In crown 8vo. **1/6**

FOUR-MINUTE SPEED TESTS. The speeds range from 80-140 words
a minute. In crown 8vo. **1/6**

SEVEN-MINUTE SPEED TESTS. In crown 8vo. **1/6**

PUBLIC EXAMINATION SPEED TESTS. The speeds range from 50-
160 words a minute. In crown 8vo. **2/-**

HIGH SPEED IN PITMAN SHORTHAND. By K. S. AIYAR, B.A.
In crown 8vo. **2/-**

CUMULATIVE SPELLER AND SHORTHAND VOCABULARY. By
CHARLES E. SMITH. In crown 8vo, cloth **2/-**

SHORTHAND SPEED CLASS. By J. C. COSTELLO. In crown 8vo . **6d.**

SPEED PRACTICE. In crown 8vo. **2/-**

SPEED TRAINING IN PITMAN'S SHORTHAND. By T. F. MARRINER.
A twelve weeks' Course of study and speed practice . . . . **6d.**

ACQUISITION OF SPEED IN SHORTHAND. By E. A. COPE. In
ordinary print. In crown 8vo **1/-**

**THEORY TESTS IN PITMAN'S SHORTHAND (First and Second
Series).** For Advanced, Theory, and Speed classes, with Key.
In crown 8vo . . . . **8d.**

**MISCELLANEOUS DICTATION TESTS FOR SHORTHAND STU-
DENTS.** In crown 8vo. **2/-**

BROWN'S SHORT-CUTS IN SHORTHAND. By GEORGE BROWN,
F.I.P.S. In crown 8vo. **1/-**

SHORTHAND COMMERCIAL LETTER-WRITER. Advanced Style **1/6**
Key **1/-**

THE SHORTHAND COMMERCIAL LETTER-WRITER AND KEY,
in one volume . . . . Cloth **2/6**

COMMERCIAL CORRESPONDENCE IN SHORTHAND. Advanced
Style. In crown 8vo . . . . Cloth **3/6**

BUSINESS CORRESPONDENCE IN SHORTHAND. Advanced Style **1/6**
Key **1/-**

TRADE CORRESPONDENCE IN SHORTHAND. Advanced Style . **1/3**
Key **1/-**

ONE-SESSION DICTATION BOOK **1/-**

**MISCELLANEOUS CORRESPONDENCE IN PITMAN'S SHORT-
HAND.** First, Second, Third, and Fourth Series. Advanced Style
with Keys in ordinary print. Each in crown 8vo, oblong . . **1/6**

BRIEF REPORTING EXERCISES IN PITMAN'S SHORTHAND.
Consisting of Exercises in Advanced Phraseography, with Key
counted in 10's for dictation. In crown 8vo **1/6**

BALANCED OUTLINES IN PITMAN'S SHORTHAND (Second Series) **6d.**

FACILITY NOTEBOOK FOR SHORTHAND STUDENTS. A notebook
with lines of shorthand for copying. 5 in. by 8 in. . . . **6d.**

THE PRACTICAL PHRASER. By JAMES HYNES. A series of phrase-
writing exercises in shorthand only. Advanced Style. 5¼ in by
7 in. **1/-**

2

PITMAN'S SHORTHAND READING BOOKS

In the Elementary Style.

A RACE AGAINST TIME, AND OTHER STORIES . . . . 9d.
READING LESSONS, No. 1 . . . . 8d.
Key . . . . 4d.
SHORT STORIES. Vols. I and II. A collection of interesting tales
                                                       Each 9d.

In the Intermediate Style.

READING LESSONS, No. 2 . . . . 8d.
Key . . . . 4d.
PITMAN'S SHORTHAND READER, No. 1. Containing extracts from
    standard authors, including Shakespeare, Charles Lamb, Hazlitt,
    Wordsworth, Pope, Kingsley, and Ruskin. With Key in ordinary
    print . . . . 8d.
TALKS ON COMMERCIAL TOPICS. By W. J. WESTON, M.A., B.Sc.
    A specially suitable reader for Commercial Students. In crown 8vo 1/–
THE BATTLE OF LIFE. By CHARLES DICKENS. Cloth . . . 2/6
TALES AND SKETCHES. By WASHINGTON IRVING; with Key in
    ordinary print 2/–
A DAUGHTER OF THE REGIMENT, AND OTHER STORIES. Three
    stories by various authors 1/–
THE COBBLER, AND OTHER STORIES. Three stories by various
    authors 1/–
GULLIVER'S VOYAGE TO LILLIPUT. By JONATHAN SWIFT . 1/6
                                                 Cloth 2/–
ALICE IN WONDERLAND. By LEWIS CAROLL 2/–

In the Advanced Style.

READING LESSONS, No. 3 . . . . 8d.
Key . . . . 4d.
PITMAN'S SHORTHAND READER II. Containing extracts from
    Addison, Dickens, Robert Louis Stevenson, Wordsworth, George
    Eliot, etc. Key in ordinary print . . . . 8d.
VARIED SHORTHAND READINGS. A collection of literary extracts.
    Crown 8vo. 1/4
SHORTHAND READING EXERCISES IN BUSINESS CORRESPOND-
    ENCE. Size, 7 in. by 5 in. 1/–
Key, counted for Dictation . . . . 10d.
HALF HOURS WITH POPULAR AUTHORS. Compiled by A.
    JEFFREY MUNRO. Vols. I, II, III, and IV . . . . Each 1/–
READINGS FROM POPULAR AUTHORS. Compiled by A. JEFFREY
    MUNRO. A delightful introduction to modern and classical literature.
    Vols. I, II, III, and IV . . . . Each 1/–
A CHRISTMAS CAROL. By CHARLES DICKENS 1/3
                                                   Cloth 2/–
TALES FROM DICKENS. Containing "The Tuggs's at Ramsgate,"
    "The Bloomsbury Christening," "The Great Winglebury Duel,"
    and "Mr. Watkins Tottle," from *Sketches by Boz.* Seventeen
    illustrations by P. Hudson. Cloth 2/6
THE STRANGE CASE OF DR. JEKYLL AND MR. HYDE. By
    ROBERT LOUIS STEVENSON 1/6
                                                   Cloth 2/–
THE SIGN OF FOUR. By Sir A. CONAN DOYLE. A complete
    Phonographic transcript of the famous "Sherlock Holmes" novel
                                                   Cloth 2/6
SELECTED EXTRACTS FROM FAVOURITE AUTHORS. Compiled
    by A. JEFFREY MUNRO. Vols. I, II, III, and IV . . Each 1/–

THE RETURN OF SHERLOCK HOLMES. By Sir A. CONAN DOYLE.
In three vols. Each cloth 2/6
TALES OF ADVENTURE AND MEDICAL LIFE. By SIR A. CONAN
DOYLE 1/3
THANKFUL BLOSSOM. By BRET HARTE . . . 2/-
KEYNOTES OF SUCCESS. In shorthand and letterpress . 1/-
SELECTIONS FROM AMERICAN AUTHORS. With Key in ordinary
print 1/6
THE LEGEND OF SLEEPY HOLLOW. By WASHINGTON IRVING.
With Key in ordinary print . . . . . 9d.
RIP VAN WINKLE. By WASHINGTON IRVING. With Key in ordinary
print. Three illustrations . . . . . 8d.
WAR OF INDEPENDENCE. By JOHN FISKE . . . 2/6
THE SILENT JUDGE AND OTHER STORIES. By MAXWELL CROOKS 1/-
RANDOM REFLECTIONS. By HAROLD DOWNS. With letterpress
Key. Crown 8vo 1/-
GARDEN OF THE SOUL. In Pitman's Shorthand, freely vocalized
and beautifully reproduced. Compiled from authorized sources.
Centenary Edition. In cloth gilt, 5 in. by 3 in. . . 3/6
THE BOOK OF PSALMS. From the Authorized Version of the Bible.
Crown 8vo, cloth gilt, red edges 3/6
NEW TESTAMENT IN SHORTHAND. Authorized Version. Cloth gilt 6/-
Roan gilt 7/6

FOREIGN ADAPTATIONS OF PITMAN'S SHORTHAND

FRENCH PHONOGRAPHY. By T. A. REED. Rules in English;
Examples, etc., in French. Fourth Edition . . . 2/-
FRENCH SHORTHAND COMMERCIAL CORRESPONDENCE. By
T. A. REED. With a Key. Cloth 1/6
STENOGRAPHIE PITMAN. By SPENCER HERBERT. . Cloth. 3/-
HOW TO ADAPT PITMAN'S SHORTHAND TO FRENCH. By W. H.
OLLIVE. In foolscap 4to . . . . . Net 1/-
CORRESPONDENCE COMMERCIALE EN STENOGRAPHIE PITMAN.
By SPENCER HERBERT. Cloth 3/-
GERMAN SHORTHAND. In German and English. Cr. 8vo. Cloth 4/-
LATIN PHONOGRAPHY. By Rev. W. TATLOCK, S. J. Rules in Latin
Cloth 2/6
SPANISH SHORTHAND. In Spanish. Fifth Edition. Rules in Spanish
Cloth 3/6
Key 2/6
SPANISH SHORTHAND DICTIONARY. Crown 8vo. . Cloth 7/6
TAQUIGRAFIA ESPANOLA CORRESPONDENCIA. Commercial
Correspondence Exercises . . . . . Cloth 1/6
WELSH SHORTHAND. In Welsh. Third Edition . . 2/-
GAELIC SHORTHAND. In crown 8vo, cloth . . . 2/6
AFRIKAANSE SHORTHAND. In crown 8vo. Second Edition. Cloth 7/6
Key 3/6
AFRIKAANSE SHORTHAND DICTATION BOOK. By A. GELDEN-
HUYS. In crown 8vo 2/-
ITALIAN SHORTHAND. By P. P. DE CESARE. In crown 8vo . 3/6

SHORTHAND TEACHERS' BOOKS

PITMAN'S SHORTHAND AND ENGLISH. By W. F. DINGWALL,
M.A., and J. HYNES. Crown 8vo. . . . .Cloth 2/6
NOTES OF LESSONS ON PITMAN'S SHORTHAND. By J. E.
McLACHLAN. Crown 8vo. . . . . .Cloth 2/6
**THE SHORTHAND TEACHER'S EXAMINATION: HOW TO
PREPARE FOR.** By J. E. McLACHLAN. Crown 8vo. . .Cloth 2/6

A COMMENTARY ON PITMAN'S SHORTHAND. For Advanced
Students and Teachers. By J. W. TAYLOR 5/-
PRINCIPLES OF TEACHING APPLIED TO PITMAN'S SHORTHAND
By R. W. HOLLAND, O.B.E., M.A., M.Sc., LL.D. In crown 8vo
Cloth 2/6
**TIPS TO TEACHERS OF PITMAN'S SHORTHAND AND OTHER
COMMERCIAL SUBJECTS.** By J. HYNES. Crown 8vo. . . 1/-
CHART OF THE PHONOGRAPHIC ALPHABET. 22 in. × 35 in. . 2d.
**DERIVATIVE AND COMPOUND WORDS IN PITMAN'S SHORT-
HAND.** By W. H. B. WILSON 2/-

SHORTHAND STATIONERY

*In ordering through a bookseller, state particularly " Fono" series
and the register number which is printed on each copy.*

No. 1.—80 pp., red lines, suitable for pen or pencil; with the
Grammalogues printed inside the cover . . . Price **2d.**
By post **3d.**; six copies, by post, **1s. 3d.**
No. 2.—140 pp., red lines, suitable for pen or pencil; with the
Grammalogues inside the cover . . . . Price **3d.**
By post **4d.**; six copies, by post, **1s. 11d.**
No. 3.—180 pp., with the Contracted Words inside the cover. . Price **5d.**
By post, **6½d.**
No. 4.—90 pp., superior paper, elastic back, flat opening . . Price **4d.**
By post, **5d.**
No. 4a.—180 pp., superior paper, elastic binding; with List of Long-
hand Press Contractions and Press Telegraph Regulations
printed inside the cover. By post, **9d.** . . . Price **7d.**
No. 5.—180 pp., 8 in. × 5 in., elastic binding to open flat or stitched
By post, **10d.** Single lines . . . . . Price **8d.**
No. 5W.—180 pp., 8 in. × 5 in. Wider lines and red ruling. By
post, **10d.**. . . . . Price **8d.**
No. 19.—140 pp., 9 in. × 4¾ in., superior paper, red lines, red marginal
lines . . . . Price **8d.**
By post, **10d.** This notebook forms a refill to Pitman's
Notebook Cover and Transcribing Slope.
No. 20.—200 pp., 8½ in. × 5½ in., elastic binding, single lines, stiff
boards, marginal red lines . . . . . Price **1/-**
By post, **1s. 3d.**
No. 21.—"S.-O.," 180 pp., 8 in. × 5 in., elastic binding, single lines,
side opening. By post, **11d.** . . . . . Price **9d.**
SHORTHAND NOTEBOOK, No. 22.—Size 8½ in. × 5½ in., 156 pp.
By post, **6½d.** . . . . Price **4d.**
NOTEBOOK COVER AND TRANSCRIBING SLOPE, 9 in. × 5 in.,
cloth. This cover folds back and, being kept at the required
angle by a piece of elastic, remains in a convenient position for
transcribing . . . . Price **2/6**
Including Notebook, **3s. 2d.**; by post, **3s. 5d.**
Refills, price **8d.**; by post, **10d.**

PENS, PENCILS, ETC.

PITMAN'S "FONO" FOUNTAIN PEN, No. 3 (Mottled Brown). 14-
carat Solid Gold Nib Iridium tipped, Box Lever Filling Device.
Pocket Safety Clip and Rolled Gold Bands. . . . **15/-**
PITMAN'S "FONO" LEVER SELF-FILLING FOUNTAIN PEN. . **7/6**
With rolled gold band and larger nib **10/6**
PITMAN'S "FONO" PENCIL . . . . . Each **2d.**
SPECIAL SHORTHAND PENCIL. . . . . Each **4d.**

TYPEWRITING WORKS

PITMAN'S COMMERCIAL TYPEWRITING. By W. and E. WALMSLEY.
Large post 4to . . . . . . Cloth **5/-**

BUSINESS TYPEWRITING. By F. HEELIS. Large post 4to . . **2/-**

PITMAN'S KEYBOARD MASTERY COURSE. By MAXWELL CROOKS.
The book is prepared for use with Pitman's *Gramophone Course of
Keyboard Instruction.* Large post 4to **1/6**

**PITMAN'S GRAMOPHONE COURSE OF TYPEWRITER KEY-
BOARD INSTRUCTION.** Complete, in strong case, together with
one copy of Instruction Book. Comprising twelve 10 in. records
(six discs) . . . . **Net 35/-**

TOUCH TYPEWRITING FOR TEACHERS. By MAXWELL CROOKS
Demy 8vo, cloth . . . . **Net 7/6**

TYPIST'S COMPANION, THE. By MAXWELL CROOKS. Crown 8vo
cloth . . . . **Net 2/-**

TOUCH TYPEWRITING MADE EASY. By G. B. WRIGHT. Large
post 4to **2/6**

TOUCH TYPEWRITING EXERCISES. By T. J. SIMONS, F.C.T.S.,
F.I.P.S. Large post 4to **1/6**

THE JUNIOR TYPIST. By ANNIE E. DAVIS. Demy 8vo, cloth.
Second Edition, Revised . . . . . . **Net 2/6**

NEW COURSE IN TYPEWRITING. By Mrs. SMITH-CLOUGH.
Large post 4to. Second Edition, Revised . . . **2/-**

A TYPEWRITING CATECHISM. By Mrs. SMITH-CLOUGH. Large
post 4to. Fifth Edition. Revised . . . . **Net 5/-**

PITMAN'S TYPEWRITER MANUAL. Can be used with any machine.
Seventh Edition. Large post 4to . . . . Cloth **5/-**

PITMAN'S EXERCISES AND TESTS IN TYPEWRITING. Compiled
and arranged by W. WALMSLEY. Fcap. folio. Third Edition . **4/-**

ADVANCED TYPEWRITING. By F. HEELIS . . . **3/6**

PRACTICAL COURSE IN TOUCH TYPEWRITING. By C. E. SMITH.
English Edition, Revised and Enlarged . . . **2/-**
Spanish Edition **2/6**

TYPEWRITER KEYBOARD CHARTS . . . **Each 3d.**

MODERN TYPEWRITING AND MANUAL OF OFFICE PROCEDURE.
By A. E. MORTON. 6½ in. by 9½ in. Twelfth Edition Cloth . **5/6**

DICTIONARY OF TYPEWRITING. (H. ETHERIDGE). Third Edition
revised by MAXWELL CROOKS and F. DAWSON, F.C.T.S. Demy
8vo, cloth **6/-**

R.S.A. TYPEWRITING TESTS. By A. E. MORTON. Three books,
Each in foolscap folio **2/6**

HIGH SPEED IN TYPEWRITING. By A. M. KENNEDY and F.
JARRETT. Demy 4to . . . . . . **Net 2/6**

"FONO" LETTER-HEADINGS FOR TYPEWRITING STUDENTS . **1/-**

**QUESTIONS AND ANSWERS ON TYPEWRITING AND OFFICE
PROCEDURE.** By ARTHUR E. MORTON. Large post 4to, cloth, **7/6**

THE BOOK OF THE UNDERWOOD TYPEWRITER. By MAXWELL
CROOKS. Crown 8vo. . . . . . . **Net 2/6**

THEORY OF TYPEWRITING. By FLORENCE LOCKEY. Large Post 4to. **6/-**

DUPLICATING AND COPYING PROCESSES. By W. DESBOROUGH,
O.B.E., F.C.I. Demy 8vo, cloth gilt . . . . **Net 5/-**

PITMAN'S TIKSKRIF. By J. E. W. BEYER, P.C.T., F.C.T.S., and
G. P. SCHEEPERS, B.A., B.C.D. In foolscap folio . . **Net 7/-**

TOETSBORDKURSUS (AFRIKAANSE TYPEWRITING EXERCISES).
By J. E. W. BEYER, P.C.T., F.C.T.S., and G. P. SCHEEPERS, B.A.,
B.C.D. Demy 4to . . . . **Net 2/-**

WORKS IN ORDINARY TYPE

LIFE OF SIR ISAAC PITMAN. By ALFRED BAKER. Demy 8vo.
With many illustrations, cloth **5/-**

THE SHORTHAND WRITER. By T. A. REED. Crown 8vo, cloth **3/6**

HISTORY OF SHORTHAND. Fourth Edition, Revised . . **6/-**

PITMAN'S COMMERCIAL TEXTBOOKS
A SELECTION

COMMERCE

COMMERCE, Stage I. By ALONZA JAMES, F.F.T.Com., F.R.Econ.S. . 2/6
COMMERCE FOR COMMERCIAL AND SECONDARY SCHOOLS. By
A. J. FAVELL, B.Sc.(Econ.), A.C.I.S. 3/6
MANUAL OF BUSINESS TRAINING. 11th Edition. By A. STEPHEN
NOEL, F.R.Econ.S. . . . . Net 4/–
BUSINESS HANDWRITING. By W. BURTON . . . . Net 1/6

ARITHMETIC

BUSINESS ARITHMETIC. Part I. Revised by IVOR T. PLANT. . 2/6
Answers . . . . Net 1/6
BUSINESS ARITHMETIC. Part II. Revised by IVOR T. PLANT. . 2/6
Answers . . . . Net 1/3
COMPLETE BUSINESS ARITHMETIC Revised by IVOR T. PLANT. 4/–
Answers . . . . Net 2/6
ARITHMETIC CLASS BOOK. By W. R. BARHAM. With Answers . 2/6

BOOK-KEEPING

SHARLES'S ELEMENTARY BOOK-KEEPING 3/6
BOOK-KEEPING STAGE I. By A. J. FAVELL, B.Sc. (Econ.), A.C.I.S. 2/6
PRINCIPLES OF ACCOUNTS, PART I. By J. STEPHENSON, M.A.,
M.Com., D.Sc. 3/6
PRINCIPLES OF ACCOUNTS, PART II. By J. STEPHENSON, M.A.,
M.Com., D.Sc. 5/–
GRADED BOOK-KEEPING EXERCISES FOR COMMERCIAL
SCHOOLS. By A. J. FAVELL 2/–

GEOGRAPHY

INTRODUCTION TO ECONOMIC GEOGRAPHY. By JAMES DAVIES. 5/–
COMMERCIAL GEOGRAPHY OF THE WORLD. By W. P. RUTTER,
M.Com. Revised Edition . . . . Net 6/–

HISTORY

COMMERCIAL HISTORY. By J. R. V. MARCHANT, M.A. . Net 5/6
THE RISE OF BRITISH COMMERCE. By K. G. LEWIS, B.A., and
N. BRANTON 3/6

COMMERCIAL CORRESPONDENCE AND ENGLISH

GUIDE TO COMMERCIAL CORRESPONDENCE AND BUSINESS
COMPOSITION. By W. J. WESTON, M.A. (Lond.). B.Sc. (Lond.) 2/6
BUSINESS LETTERS IN ENGLISH. By W. J. WESTON . . Net 3/6
COMMERCIAL CORRESPONDENCE AND COMMERCIAL ENGLISH.
Net 3/6
ENGLISH AND COMMERCIAL CORRESPONDENCE. By HIROMU
NAGAOKA AND DANIEL THEOPHILUS, B.A. 3/6

LANGUAGES

COMMERCIAL FRENCH GRAMMAR. By F. W. M. DRAPER, M.A.
Net 2/6
COMMERCIAL GERMAN GRAMMAR. By BITHELL, M.A. . Net 3/6

*For further particulars see Pitman's Commercial Catalogue, sent post free
on application to*

LONDON: SIR ISAAC PITMAN & SONS, LTD., PARKER ST., KINGSWAY, W.C.2

Pitman's Journal
OF
Commercial Education

FOUNDED BY SIR ISAAC PITMAN IN 1842

Every Saturday, 2d., by post **3d.** Monthly, in a wrapper, **10d.,** by post **1s.** Can be ordered from any Newsagent or Bookstall. Half-yearly volumes commence in April and October.

The only weekly periodical of its kind and the recognized organ of Commercial Education, now deals comprehensively with all aspects of Commercial Education, and is of maximum value to all students who are preparing for professional examinations or who are fitting themselves by self-study for responsible positions in the commercial world. Both junior and senior students are catered for, and in addition to all the popular subjects of a commercial course—Pitman's Shorthand, Typewriting, Book-keeping and Accountancy, Arithmetic, English Grammar and Composition, French, Spanish, and German, etc.—the various subjects of Professional and Secretarial Courses—Commercial Law, Company Law, Secretarial Practice, Commercial History, Commercial Geography, Psychology, Economics, Banking, Advertising Salesmanship, Shipping, and Insurance, etc.—are adequately treated in authoritative articles by experts.

Subjects of interest to commercial students and commercial and professional workers are also dealt with in leading articles and in notes, etc., and there are eight pages of printed shorthand, with key, and one page without key. "Answers to Correspondents" forms a link between students and the Editor, who is always pleased to help students to overcome their difficulties.

PITMAN'S JOURNAL OF COMMERCIAL EDUCATION can also be had by post DIRECT from the Publishers. The terms are : 3 months, by post **3s. 3d.** ; 6 months, by post **6s. 6d.** 12 months, by post, **13s.**

SIR ISAAC PITMAN & SONS, LTD., KINGSWAY, W.C.2

DEC. 33